She has made a significant contribution to our members' understanding of corporate governance and the process of buying and selling a business. She takes what is a relatively dull subject and has her audience wanting to hear her every word and debate as her lively personality, intellect, delivery and knowledge are captivating.
**Robert Drew, Chief Executive, TEC International (UK) Ltd**

Your sessions on the role of a director have been compelling. You have turned a boring and frightening subject into something that everyone can learn from. It is no wonder that we are booking you two years in advance.
**Brian Chernett, CEO, The Academy for Chief Executives**

Thank you for a fantastic session. The group scored you the highest it has ever scored anyone and were unanimous that it was the best session we have ever had. From my perspective as Chair you engaged the group well, maintained control and there was great take home value.
**Bob Battye, Group Chair, TEC International (UK) Ltd**

Feedback from delegates indicates that Jo's approach and style is refreshing and energetic in handling what can be difficult subject matter.
**Andrew Spencer, Programme Management, IoD Director of Development**

# About the author

**Jo Haigh** trained as a lawyer at the University of Leeds but changed direction early on, ultimately becoming finance director and company secretary of a public company subsidiary food group. Here she was involved in both a management buy-out and disposal to a public company, as well as several acquisitions.

On having children, she rather misguidedly believed that running her own business would give her more time, and she established a multidisciplinary consultancy which she owned for nearly ten years, holding numerous non-executive director roles. At the same time she developed a national reputation as a public speaker on corporate governance and mergers and acquisitions with the Institute of Directors and similar organisations.

Jo Haigh currently runs the corporate finance department for gvt, a firm of specialist advisers based in Yorkshire. When relaxing, she likes to travel and visit her homes in Deauville and Estapona.

# THE
# BUSINESS
# RULES

## PROTECT YOURSELF
## AND YOUR COMPANY
## FROM OVER
## 100 HIDDEN PITFALLS

## Jo Haigh

PIATKUS

Copyright © 2005 by Jo Haigh

First published in Great Britain in 2005 by
Piatkus Books Ltd
5 Windmill Street, London W1T 2JA
email: info@piatkus.co.uk

**The moral right of the author has been asserted**

*A catalogue record for this book is available from the British Library*

ISBN 0 7499 2626 0

Thanks to A P Watt Ltd on behalf of The National Trust for Places of Historic Interest and National Beauty for permission to quote 'If—' by Rudyard Kipling (from *Complete Poems: The Definitive Edition*, Doubleday, 1989)

Text design by Goldust Design
Edited by Barbara Kiser

This book has been printed on paper manufactured with respect for the environment using wood from managed sustainable resources

Typeset by Action Publishing Technology Ltd, Gloucester
Printed and bound in Great Britain by
Mackays Ltd, Chatham, Kent

For my beautiful girls
Jessica and Pollyanna

## If—

IF you can keep your head when all about you
Are losing theirs and blaming it on you,
If you can trust yourself when all men doubt you,
But make allowance for their doubting too;
If you can wait and not be tired by waiting,
Or being lied about, don't deal in lies,
Or being hated, don't give way to hating,
And yet don't look too good, not talk too wise:

If you can dream – and not make dreams your master;
If you can think – and not make thoughts your aim;
If you can meet with Triumph and Disaster
And treat those two impostors just the same;
If you can bear to hear the truth you've spoken
Twisted by knaves to make a trap for fools,
Or watch the things you gave your life to, broken,
And stoop and build 'em up with worn-out tools:

If you can make one heap of all your winnings
And risk it on one turn of pitch-and-toss,
And lose, and start again at your beginnings
And never breathe a word about your loss;
If you can force your heart and nerve and sinew
To serve your turn long after they are gone,
And so hold on when there is nothing in you
Except the Will which says to them: 'Hold on!'

If you can talk with crowds and keep your virtue,
Or walk with Kings – nor lose the common touch,
If neither foes nor loving friends can hurt you,
If all men count with you, but none too much;
If you can fill the unforgiving minute
With sixty seconds' worth of distance run,
Yours is the Earth and everything that's in it,
And – which is more – you'll be a Man, my son!

**Rudyard Kipling**

# Contents

# Acknowledgements

This book would never have happened without the help of a number of people. It is impossible to name them all, but I would like to thank the following.

My husband Mike, for believing in me and giving me constant support (I couldn't have done it without you, darling), my children Jessica and Pollyanna and my step-children Katie and David, who are so proud of me – however misguided that might be!

My brilliantly supportive friends and colleagues at gvt, in particular Claire, Keith and Melanie for their wisdom and input and Mark for giving me encouragement at all the appropriate moments.

My PA Natalie, whose ability to read my appalling scrawl has meant the first versions of the book were at least readable – Nat, you were indispensable.

Roger at HLW for his generosity in proofreading the final draft and correcting me in his own inimitable fashion – Roger, you are so one of my favourite solicitors – and also many thanks to Keith Arrowsmith at HLW for his inside tips.

And finally, all the fantastic people at Piatkus, who believed in me when I almost gave up after draft four million and one!

# Foreword

It is refreshing to support a book that is so practical and has everyday use. Jo Haigh brings her experience to this book advising all those involved with starting, running and selling a company on a list of serious business considerations that must be taken into account. The messages in this book are not an option; they encompass the complete set of requirements to run a business effectively. It is laced with great ideas and cautionary notes on how to effectively govern the business from the start until its eventual sale. Jo Haigh is a valued and recognised speaker to over 650 of our chief executive members and is called back many times to build on their knowledge. This book is a 'must have' reference book for all companies. I endorse it wholeheartedly.

Robert S Drew, Chief Executive TEC International – The Global Leader in Chief Executive Development

# Why you need this book

It has been said that we are a nation of shopkeepers – 75 per cent of businesses in the UK are privately owned, with the largest proportion of these owned and managed by the same people. By that I mean that the shareholders and the directors are one and the same.

If this sounds like you, your business may have begun with an inheritance, a desire to improve your lifestyle or simply to make a living. But whatever the reason, and whether you are in the early stages of the business life cycle or well entrenched, it is unlikely that you will be fully aware of exactly what you should be doing, why and when – or what the ramifications of getting it wrong might be.

In this book I want to draw your attention to the many pitfalls that lie in wait if you own, manage or run your own business. Here I give you advice that you may not find easily elsewhere, as you often aren't aware of what you don't know and therefore don't know what questions you should be asking. This advice may not be easily available if you run a small company without the benefit of a financial or legal director.

I trained as a lawyer and subsequently became a financial director and company secretary of a major subsidiary of a public company. In my work consulting to businesses big and small, I am constantly concerned by the lack of knowledge of many of the people I meet. This book is written as a direct response to the issues I encounter every week.

My aim in writing this book is to alert you to aspects of running a business that you may well not be aware of, to save you time and money, and to give you peace of mind.

Companies House, the official UK register of UK companies,

lists millions of directors. And there are at least the same number of people acting as directors, with all the incumbent liabilities. Yet they may not even know they are directors – yes, you can be a director without being registered as such!

This is not simply a guide on how to comply with legislation to get it right (although the book certainly covers some of that); nor is it meant only to be read by directors. This book is intended for anyone and everyone who is, or has aspirations to be, involved in the world of business, in a small to medium-sized enterprise.

It is by no means a textbook and is not meant to replace professional advice. Rather, it's a way of giving you insights into the complex, diverse and changing world of entrepreneurial activity.

Some things will shock and surprise you, some will seem totally unfair. Others you may have some knowledge of. However the book strikes you, you will undoubtedly come away from it with a greater understanding of self preservation and corporate protection.

It is certain that if you even attempted to comply with and adhere to all these principles in practice, you might be left wondering where you were supposed to find the time to run your company. But this book will at least help you to develop a sense of awareness and build the all-important fireguards round your brazier.

And that is a vital step. The rules of corporate governance and the role of the director change almost daily, and it is highly probable that you will not have a chance of keeping up to date. However, some principles are cast in stone and if you want to turn a poor company into a good one or a good one into a great one, this book provides you with firm footing.

As you read this book, you may find that some of the issues discussed frighten you to death. In fact, you will be amazed at what you didn't know you didn't know, and the extent of the personal and professional liabilities this could create for you. Remember, ignorance of the law is simply not an excuse. Working on the principle that over 2,000 directors a year are being disqualified and this number is increasing year on year, it's worth at least trying to act with a degree of compliance.

Lots – and I mean lots – of people have aspirations to run their own company and to take up board positions, but many of them lack any real comprehension of what that actually means. Before making an appointment to your board or taking up the appointment you have been offered, read this book and make a more informed choice. At the very least you will know what you don't know!

## How to use this book

In structuring this book, we have tried to consider the critical areas involved in creating and running a business, from the initial stages of structuring the company and some first-stage basic arrangements, through to understanding the pitfalls and advantages of a well-constructed exit.

Within each of these sections, for ease of identification, we have listed areas of interest in alphabetical order.

The first time you read this book, a thorough cover-to-cover perusal will give you an excellent overall understanding of the good, bad and frankly scary aspects of owning, managing and running your own business. But it can also be used as a quick reference guide, and is an absolute must for those moments when you encounter an unfamiliar situation. Do remember that you should always obtain professional business advice – this book is not intended to be a substitute for it.

You'll find a glossary of basic terms at the back of the book. Lawyers and accountants like to confuse the innocent by using technical terms – so this will come in very handy.

You may also like to start the whole process by completing the 'who wants to be a director' quiz on page 200 to gauge how much you know. Be aware, however, that this doesn't replace personal professional counsel, and that you're well advised to always seek this before you make any firm decisions or commitments.

Note that as of April 2005, the UK's Inland Revenue and H M Customs & Excise have been replaced by H M Revenue & Customs (HMRC), so in this book I make no reference to the two former government departments.

# Structure:
# the basic concepts

CORPORATION, n. An ingenious device for obtaining individual profit without individual responsibility.
**Ambrose Bierce, *The Devil's Dictionary***

With most things, if you get it right first time it will save you a lot of heartache, as well as time and money, later on. Establishing your business is no exception.

What you'll find is that many of the problems you encounter will arrive at a stage in your business cycle when – more often than not – the various parties involved are at loggerheads, if not actually at war. Negotiating in this arena is therefore bound to be more complex (and for complex, read expensive!).

It's perfectly possible, however, to set up a company for a modest £100. There are any number of firms, including specialist businesses, whose job it is to create companies. The trick is starting as you mean to continue.

This section of the book deals with the preliminaries – the things you need to sort out at the beginning of your new venture. But having said that, better late than never. So if after reading this, you realise there are some glaring omissions in your setup, don't panic: instead, gear up for action.

# Group effort

It's particularly important to address any outstanding issues in your fledgling business when all is bright and cheerful in the camp, as it's always easier to sort things out when all the parties involved are still friends! So sit down with your colleagues and get going on the issues, one by one.

No business is an island, so looking further afield for ideas and advice is always useful. Look at other businesses, and talk to friends and colleagues to find out what has worked and not worked for them. Thus you'll have the opportunity to learn from their mistakes.

It can also be hugely helpful to bring in outside help, wherever you are in the process. Don't be tempted to cut corners here unless your business aspirations are very modest (and I presume you wouldn't have purchased this book if that were the case). You are going to have to spend a little cash on professional help and advice, but it will be money well spent, I promise you.

# What price advice?

If costs are of concern in seeking help from other professionals – and let's face it, no one wants to pay too much for advice – try Business Link (their website is at www.businesslink.gov.uk, or call 0845 600 9 006) or your trade federation, who may be able to provide discounts.

If this is not available, ask for quotes from your advisers. Obviously, cheapest isn't always the best; but do get comparisons and certainly make sure you use the right type of adviser. That means not only people who are used to the particular issue, but who also deal with it on a regular basis. They need to be familiar with the size of your business and even industry type – that is, the sector in which your business operates.

Changes in American legislation have meant that it is not possible for a company to use their auditors as advisers in the US. Although this is not yet a UK requirement, it is very probable that it will become law here shortly, although there will be some exemptions.

In theory at least, the US law makes sense. Auditors are the watchdog of the shareholder, while advisers are the support team for the directors, so ensuring they are separate is logical. But in practice, it will probably mean an increase in total costs. My advice is simply to buy the best advice you can afford.

We are becoming, as a society, more litigious (as you will see as you read further!), so costs spent at the start of your venture will almost certainly help limit them when things go wrong.

## Keeping track of changes

As your enterprise progresses, your requirements will change and you may need to revisit some of the basic documentation you and your advisers have put together – so don't lose it! That may sound silly, but unless you keep track of these documents or place them with your accountant or solicitor (probably the safest bet), chances are you will lose them just when you need to find them urgently.

You also need to keep up with the changing shape of business itself. Historically, the only way to do business was as a sole trader or a partnership. Then, in the late 19th century, along came the concept of a limited liability company. Since then any number of other types of businesses have been created, both by statute and European directives. October 2004 saw the advent of a new entity, the European registered company (known as Societas Europea), while Community Interest Companies and Public Benefit Corporations showed up in 2005.

These models, along with joint ventures and special purpose vehicles, give you opportunities for exploring different corporate possibilities, some of which may be more appropriate to your needs than others. Make sure your advisers keep you up to date on changes and opportunities, as there will be all sorts of implications arising from not choosing the right model, not least of which is a personal liability.

Let me give you a couple of examples. If you establish as a partnership or sole trader, you'll have less protection from personal actions by creditors, but better cash flow at the start of running your business. With a company, on the other hand, you may have to pay yourself a salary and so pay income tax as you go along – which isn't great for cash flow – but you can at least be sure that only on rare occasions can a creditor sue you directly.

Clearly, you need to understand the pros and cons of each type of business entity before choosing one or another.

## Structure checklist

So what do you need to do to structure a business?

1. Find out about the different types of business entities that exist. Don't just assume you need a company limited by shares or a partnership – check out the various options, ask for information on the pros and cons for your type of trade and circumstances, talk to friends, colleagues, your bank manager and professional advisers.

2. Select the appropriate model for your business type.

3. Put in place some 'ground rules'. This section of the book will help with this, but you'll need shareholders' agreements (if you form a company) or partnership agreements if you choose that route, job descriptions and contracts of employment, and some basic financial management tools for checking and monitoring your performance.

4. Choose a suitable accountant and solicitor. Don't just select on price; choose on reputation and relevant skills, and agree terms.

5. Get the **right** funding in place (see 'Funding: the ins and outs of raising money', starting on page 46) and stick to the terms of the deal.

6. Plan your exit! (Yes, I did say exit.) This might seem startling

at the moment, but you must plan for this right at the beginning to ensure you maximise business value (see 'Exiting: getting out gracefully', starting on page 183).

7. Research your market and customers thoroughly. Don't try to sell what people don't want – however much you happen to want it.

8. Check and recheck your costings and prices and keep doing that. 'Me too' business rarely succeeds.

In essence, therefore, the key to structure is to give very careful consideration to what suits you best – in all possible ways. You will then get your business off to the right start.

In the text that follows, you'll find that not everything is immediately relevant to you right now. Note, however, that each section does contain areas that will need your consideration at some stage in the development of your business.

# 1. Agents and distributors

I rate enthusiasm even above professional skill.
**Sir Edward Appleton, English Atmospheric Physicist and Nobel Prize winner 1947**

You need people to sell your product. But do they need to be part of your permanent staff? Not always. One way of potentially increasing your sales, without the cost of a fixed overhead in the guise of a sales force, is to use third parties who are only paid on their performance.

You must ensure that the people you hire to do this job aren't **potential employees**, however. Under Inland Revenue guidelines, third party suppliers, if not treated in the appropriate manner, can be classed as staff.[*1]

[*1] See Compliance, section 16, p. 106

Such personnel can be termed either agents or distributors and are likely to provide their services to several companies simultaneously. There is, however, a fundamental difference between the role of agent and that of distributor.

A distributor is simply buying the goods from you, and it is up to them whether, and at what value, they sell them on. An agent, on the other hand, will not buy the goods from you but will merely negotiate the sale for you to another third party.

Before 1994, the relationship you established with your agent was up to the parties involved, but the European Directive that came into place on 1 January 1994 provided a series of minimum requirements for agency relationships, covering standard commissions calculations, termination rights and payment periods.

For distributors, there is very little protection unless a specific contractual agreement is drawn up, so ensuring that the business relationship between you and your distributor is crystal-clear is important for all parties.

Unsurprisingly, a written contract is the best way to ensure this. (Hollywood mogul Sam Goldwyn, after all, said that 'a verbal contract isn't worth the paper it is written on'!) The contract should detail such matters as exclusivity of distribution, the period of the agreement and termination rights, along with general terms on payment, marketing, stock availability and so on.

It should also set out specifics on pricing and retention of title rights, confidentiality and dispute issues – for instance, if you wish matters of disagreement to be dealt with by arbitration in the first place, you must state this.

Finally, one area often overlooked is the value of any intellectual property that resides in the products being traded. There have been a number of successful cases that have seen the distributor gain ownership of the goodwill residing in a brand because of a poor-quality agreement. (Goodwill is the worth over and above the value of the tangible assets themselves.) So it is essential to ensure that you retain control over packaging, branding and the like to protect your ownership.

# 2. All in a name

In this age, which believes that there is a short cut to
everything, the greatest lesson to be learned is that the
most difficult way is, in the long run, the easiest.
**Henry Miller, *The Books in My Life***

Are you absolutely sure that the company name on your cheque-
book is exactly the same as the name registered at Companies
House? And I mean **exactly**:
• Same spelling
• ( ) in the right place
• Limited or Ltd
• Singular or plural
• Upper v lower case
• And v &

If it isn't, every cheque you issue is regarded as a personal
cheque of the directors. That means that if the bank doesn't
honour the cheque, for whatever reason, you may have to!

Recently I encountered an example of this problem. The company's
name was registered as Xyz Building Merchants Limited – but the name
on the chequebook was Xwz Builders Merchants Limited!

So be aware that in business, 'What's in a name?' is a loaded question.

# 3. Appointment, remuneration and removal of directors

*When a man tells you that he got rich through hard work, ask him: 'Whose?'*
**Don Marquis, writer, poet and New York columnist**

In a private limited company you must have at least one director (plus a company secretary). In a public company the requirement is two. Of course, you can have more, and often there will be no maximum number allowed – you will find this information in your Articles of Association.

These are part of the constitutional documents you must have when setting up your company. The Articles tell you how your directors must behave – read them with a strong cup of coffee! (And don't forget that you also need a Memorandum of Association – documents that basically tell you what your company can and cannot do.)

When you appoint a director, you will need to send form 288a to Companies House. This form should be signed by an existing director and the new appointee.

People over the age of 70 cannot be directors without special permission in the Articles; nor can your auditor sit on your board as a director.

If you become sectioned under the Mental Health Act or are just absent from board meetings (without permission) for six months or more, you will also be disqualified from taking up a position as a director. Note that this does not include compassionate leave or sick leave, though it may depend on your particular terms of employment.

One client appointed a director from the local 'great and good', and told him not to bother to attend board meetings, as they only wanted the kudos of his name. When that company failed, the judge's reprimand was very severe, and the absent director was disqualified for an extended period!

You may also be surprised that directors as such have no right to remuneration as directors unless specifically allowed in the Articles (so make sure yours have that particular provision!), although they can be paid as employees. And if you wish to provide your directors with a service contract[*1] (always a good idea), this cannot exceed a five-year period unless the shareholders agree. Shareholders also have the right to inspect a director's contract.

# Exit procedures

If you want to exit your role as a director, of course you can resign just like anyone else, although it is possible that certain restrictions will be placed on your personal behaviour. For instance, you may not immediately be able to go to work for a competitor, or set up a rival company.

Nor will resignation necessarily relieve you of your liabilities or free you from certain obligations. Be aware that your liability remains with you for three years after you resign and of course indefinitely for fraud and criminal related activities. That means that the ramifications of any decisions that you participate in while still in office will be just as much your problem as it is of those directors who still hold the role.

Usually, the standard procedure in the Articles is for shareholders to remove directors, but yours may not have the standard format, and some Articles allow specific shareholders or classes of shareholders to remove directors. The board itself does not normally have the right to remove a director from office as a director, but can remove a director as an employee.

The removal of a director from the office of director requires an

[*1] See Structure, section 8, p. 19

ordinary resolution (that means that 51 per cent of the voting shareholders must agree). The company is given 28 days' notice and the director in question must be informed, and has a right to either speak personally to the meeting or make a written representation. Either way, the director may well have an unfair dismissal claim related to his employment status, so advice on proceeding correctly must be taken from a qualified person such as your solicitor or a representative of ACAS, the employee relations body.

For more on exiting, see 'Exiting: getting out gracefully', page 183.

# 4. Board and quorums

A Board – A body that takes minutes and wastes hours.
**Milton Berle, Jewish American comedian**

As you'll know, a board of directors is a group of people chosen by your shareholders to promote their interests. But you may not know whether the decisions your board are making are valid. Be aware that any resolution passed at a board meeting at which the required quorum is not present may be invalid.

What's the required quorum? You will find your standard quorum number in your Articles of Association. Most private companies who use the standard Memorandum and Articles of Association (your constitutional documents provided to you when you incorporate) as laid out in the Companies Act have a default quorum of two, and usually this requires a person to be physically present.

It is possible to have telephone or video conference board meetings but you should probably have a specific provision in your Articles to allow for this.

It is also possible to pass a resolution validly if **all** directors sign a written resolution.

Quorums can be varied, but if you want to change your Articles you will need to pass a special resolution – a vote by your share-holders – and you will need 75 per cent of them to agree to this.

You can be quite specific about your quorum. For instance, you can insist that it includes particular directors (by title), such as the managing director or chairman.

If you hold a meeting that isn't quorate, it may be possible to validate the decisions made at a later stage, when a quorum does exist; but this clearly isn't really best practice.

## Improving accountability

You may also like to think about other governance issues to improve accountability, such as:

- Notice periods for meetings (don't forget a short-notice provision).
- Minutes and distribution of information pre and post-meeting.

Such procedures will not only improve your general effectiveness, but will protect you from your fellow directors acting without you if you also ensure you must be present to guarantee a valid decision. As the Companies Act contains no special provisions for the way directors' meetings must be held, decisions are binding if made on a simple majority, including alternate directors (those standing in place of an absent director or indeed shadow directors). So great care must be taken with these governance issues.

For instance, you might own all the shares, but if you have appointed other directors, they may be able to out-vote you at a board meeting unless you amend the constitution so that only resolutions which you approve are passed. Removing directors later may not be possible, as you need at least 28 days' notice.

Don't forget: ignorance is never an excuse, and directors have a duty to ensure they are fully aware of all the decisions taken. Make sure you have a system that ensures you are informed and involved.

Minutes and records of meetings are an excellent source of

evidence in a controversial or even litigious situation – keep a signed copy of board minutes at home!

# 5. Corporate governance

What is a committee? A group of the unwilling, picked from the unfit, to do the unnecessary.
**Richard Harkness, American TV news and radio commentator**

The essence of corporate governance is about acting properly with both integrity and care. We can see the importance of this through what happens when corporate governance falters. The increasing number of high-profile business failures on both sides of the Atlantic have shaken public confidence and left shareholders, employees and creditors with huge, unrecoverable losses.

Good governance isn't simply about legislation. It's also about good practice, and a large number of reports have recognised this. Indeed, these have culminated in the production of The Combined Code, a code of good practice primarily for publicly quoted companies but hugely relevant for all businesses in terms of creating a good governance framework. (You can see a copy of the Code at www.fsa.gov.uk/pubs/ukla/lr_comcode3.pdf.)

As a new or small to medium-sized business, you may see little value in the code as such, but when looking to grow and develop a great company you'd be well advised to consider its implications.

The essence of good governance concerns transparency, accountability and probity, and when forming and acting within your board you should adhere to these principles.

Due to personal liabilities, directors should practice in accordance with principles that help protect corporate assets and, by implication, help run and manage a better business.

# Principles in practice

Here are some practical tips on governance principles:

1. Look at the composition of your board in terms of its mix of age, sex, race and so on, as well as skills and personality. A guide for board diversity can be found in the Tyson Report (available online at www.womenandequalityunit.gov.uk/publications/Tyson_report.doc or from the London Business School at www.london.edu/index.html, or call 0207 262 5050).

2. Evaluate your board's performance on a regular basis, and ensure that its members are adequately trained and supported to help them fulfil their role. (Have you noticed there is very little training about for directors? Try the Institute of Directors for starters.)

3. The Combined Code recommends the use of board committees not only to help deal with the volume of work, but also to look at a separation of powers. Although such a move isn't applicable to all companies, particularly very small businesses, as a minimum you might want to look at setting up audit, nomination and remuneration committees.

4. In looking at how the board reports to its shareholders, think clear and balanced reports available in a readable fashion – and think about the availability of a two-way communication channel. Set up a system that allows your investors not only to be talked to, but to talk to you about their concerns and ideas.

5. Risk management is fundamental to corporate governance, and is a very hot topic at the moment. Basically, it means identifying and clarifying the risks within your business, from IT to environmental issues, then ensuring you have a plan in place to manage any problems that arise. Have you got a risk strategy? How is it monitored and implemented? Check out the Combined Code for more information.

6. How do you ensure directors are acting in good faith? Think about a disclosures register to manage potential conflicts. This register will document any other directorships or shareholdings that your colleagues may have – or if you really wanted to be comprehensive, that their close family may have. This will ensure that if there is any possibility that a director is benefiting due to his relationship with the company, all parties are clearly aware of that and can act appropriately.

7. How often do you meet as a board? Good companies tend to meet once a month. However, it is the quality rather than the quantity that is important. Top of my agenda for a good meeting is the effectiveness of the chair and a strong, challenging agenda. The lack of either can make a board meeting a truly bored meeting!

8. One of the top reasons for board failure is a poorly constructed board; another is lack of quality and time-sensitive financial information. Make sure you keep good-quality minutes, and that a copy of the signed set is given to each director. This can be a very valuable source of evidence that the board has acted with care and skill at a later stage.

9. Manage your accountability by being prepared to explain what has happened if things go wrong, and what you did to put it right. Above all, accept that there is collective responsibility for your action.

10. All corporate policies are important, but some are very very important – not least your health and safety policy.[1] Make sure you keep abreast of changes, are well informed and that you liaise with your workforce on both strategic development and implementation of your health and safety policies. Above all, make sure that your board decisions reflect your health and safety intention. Directors can be criminally liable if their company breaches certain legislation, including some health and safety and environmental legislation.

---

[1] See Compliance, section 11, p. 98

These tips are not about making the board process so cumbersome that you lose sight of the purpose of the board. Rather, they're here to help you ensure your board serves its proper purpose in the best way it can.

The job of the board, remember, is to drive the strategic business of the company. As Lord Hanson said, 'If the board isn't doing that ... who is?'

There are enough 'scare stories' in the press to warn any directors – just look at Equitable Life, Enron and Xerox! Do you want to join their ranks?

# 6. Corporate variety

Choice has always been a privilege of those who could afford to pay for it.
**Ellen Frankfort, writer and 1960s feminist**

If you are going to form a company, you may as well explore all the options regarding the form your new venture will take. You may be surprised to find out there is more than one kind of entity available to you. As well as the unlimited company*1 and the unlisted PLC*2 mentioned later in this section, you could of course simply opt for a straightforward limited company; these account for the majority of registered companies in the UK.

These private limited companies must have one director and one shareholder plus a company secretary, and as long as they are classed as a small company under EU regulations – that is, the turnover must not exceed £5.6 million, the balance sheet net worth must be below £2.8 million, and there must be fewer than 50 employees – they will not need an audit.

If you choose this type of entity and it is classed as a small

---

*1 See Structure, section 20, p. 44
*2 See Structure, section 14, p. 31

company, you can, with the agreement of your shareholders, dispense with quite a lot of the formalities attached to large businesses, including laying accounts in front of the AGM or even holding an AGM. And you won't have to go through the formal process of appointing auditors.

# Beyond PLC

Another option suitable for businesses such as charities and trade associations are companies limited by guarantee. These businesses have no shareholders, but have members who provide a guarantee that if the business becomes insolvent they will make a contribution to the shortfall of any creditors. Usually this is limited to somewhere between £1 and £100 per member. In most other ways these businesses look like limited companies, as they will have boards of directors and are subject to tax (although if they are a charity, there will be various specific implications regarding tax).

Unlike a private limited company, which must use the word 'limited' in their name, companies limited by guarantee can sometimes be permitted to exclude the word.

There can be any number of members, but the membership will cease when a person dies or resigns. This differs from the case of shareholders in a private company, where the shareholding must be sold or transferred.

You may also come across companies incorporated by charter (some universities, for example, or the BBC) or those incorporated by statute such as former nationalised industries.

As of 2005, there are three new options for corporate status:

- The CIC (community interest company) is a choice for organisations wishing to use their profits for public good. These businesses, whose principal aim must be for the benefit of the community, will be regulated by a new independent regulator.
- For larger organisations, the Public Benefit Corporation will be an option. These have largely been created to give more autonomy to public sector organisations. They also will be governed by an independent specialist regulator.

- Or, by registering with the Societas Europeas (SE), which came into being in late 2004, a company can gain European status governed by European laws. The aim here is to better manage company transactions across borders, which can be confusing. Any SE-registered businesses will be held accountable under European legislation. Whichever entity you choose, the transition period can be unwieldy and expensive, so consider carefully which one best suits your purpose regarding both taxation and governance issues.

# 7. Director and officers' liability insurance

A detailed analysis of strategy usually reveals that the best time to take positive action is last year.
A. J. Carroll, *Bluff Your Way in Tax*

Directors are personally liable in a substantial number of areas, including health and safety, data protection and negligence, to name just a few! You may be able to provide yourself with an element of protection by securing some appropriate insurance.

There have been some well-publicised claims brought against directors – remember Enron, Equitable Life, Barings and Marconi? As these actions enter the public domain, your own chance of being sued probably increases.

It is a fact that we are a far more litigious country than ever before. You only have to turn on the TV to see the 'no win no fee' litigation commercials! So taking action to protect yourself from being sued and perhaps even against spurious actions – such as wholly unsubstantiated shareholder suppression claims or supplier and customer contract disputes – has become more relevant.

Cover can be provided on an individual or board basis. Do ensure that if this is a company policy, your Memorandum and Articles of Association allow for this insurance to be put in place. Otherwise you could find the policy is not valid!

It may also be possible to purchase entity cover, which provides cover for the company as well as the current board members and officers (officers being senior management or company secretaries and including shadow directors[*1]).

Regrettably, due to the increase in claims against directors, premiums have risen. So it is vital that you check the small print, as you may find there are exclusions or very specific conditions attached to making a valid claim, such as a requirement to respond to regulator enquiries or take up disciplinary proceedings.

Entity cover essentially provides insurance to protect the director or officers against any claim made against them. It pays for any costs arising from the defence of a claim, such as a duty of care or a slander action or even against wrongful trading[*2] (be sure to watch for the small print here, particularly in the latter case).

Potentially, claims can be brought by anyone, including creditors in insolvency cases. So it is well worth having this insurance in place. I find it helps me sleep a little better at night!

# 8. Directors' service contracts

I make progress by having people around who are smarter than I am and listening to them. And I assume that everyone is smarter about something than I am.
**Henry J. Kaiser, American industrialist and father of American shipbuilding**

As well as being a director, you are also an employee. And the rights and obligations attached to these two roles are separate.

[*1] See Structure, section 17, p. 37
[*2] See People and personal liabilities, section 14, p. 137

So although you will by law have to have an employment contract after eight weeks' service*[1], even an implied one (that is, one that isn't written), you don't necessarily have to have a director's service contract.

In order to protect both you and your company, however, it's a good idea to consider whether you should have such a document.

As well as the usual terms contained in an employment contract, a director's service contract is likely to include both some enhancements to certain terms, and some additional terms not usually included in a standard employment contract.

## The director's cut

A director's service contract may, for instance, contain notice periods that are more extensive than the statutory limit, which is essentially one week for every year of service up to a maximum of 12. Usually, directors have a six-month notice clause, but it could be as long as five years – although beyond this amount, you would need shareholders' approval.

Equally, the contract could be for a fixed period, or a specified period subject to notice by either party.

Some sections must be specifically included for directors. For instance, there is 'garden leave' – the right to ask a director to stay at home and not contact any company-related personnel while they are on notice. This clause will only be allowed if it is definitely specified or both parties agree to its application should the contract be silent (that is, if it doesn't mention that such a possibility is needed).

If you force a director to take pay in lieu of notice when such a clause was not in a contract, this breach could mean that the other terms of the contract may be unenforceable. As this can include restrictive covenants, this could clearly be a major issue.

One important clause would be to include the provision that should a director resign, he is also deemed to have given up his

*[1] See Compliance, section 2, p. 85

employment rights, and vice versa. This will prevent directors resigning from the board but remaining as an employee – a very difficult situation!

Apropos of this, I can recall one horror story where a particular employee who was also a director was made redundant, but refused to give up his directorship. In this case the shareholders who were not on the board also declined to be involved (citing family issues as the reason). This meant you had a very, very disgruntled director entitled to vote at meetings and so on. Soon after, of course, the business suffered – in this case, so seriously that it failed.

Restrictive covenants – agreements that restrict where a director can work or who they can work for, say after leaving your employment – can apply over more of the country or industry for a director who is also an employee, to reflect their seniority and the impact on the business if they leave. But preventing someone from earning an income may not be sustainable.

For example, a covenant that prevents an exiting director from working anywhere in the industry, in the world, would be very unlikely to be acceptable in law unless you could show that for a short period this was essential to protect the company's goodwill.

It is certain that many directors would wish to see a corporate commitment by the company to provide directors and officers with liability[*2] insurance. Such a clause would be usual in a service contract.

It would be wise also to include a confidentiality clause – that is, a provision to prevent the director disclosing sensitive confidential information – along with a non-solicitation clause, which would prevent a director poaching staff or customers.

It is recommended that a clear disciplinary policy is documented, as it is likely that this will be quite different for directors and employees.

As with any contract, once signed, the terms can only be

---

[*2] See Structure, section 7, p. 17

changed by mutual agreement. So both parties should take advice at the outset from an experienced employment lawyer.

# 9. Intellectual property

> And while the law of competition may be sometimes hard for the individual, it is best for the race, because it ensures the survival of the fittest in every department.
> **Andrew Carnegie, Scottish American businessman and philanthropist**

'Intellectual property' or IP refers to intangible creations or inventions, such as a design or published articles, which have commercial value and can be protected by legal measures such as a patent, trademark, brand, copyright or the goodwill of your business.

Because of these products' intangible nature, the methods used to protect them are different from those concerning assets you can see and touch. Ensuring you protect them in the right way will almost certainly enhance their value and your ability to trade them at a later stage. Obviously, IP protection works both ways, and you will need to take care that you are not treading on anyone else's toes, while ensuring that no one steps on yours!

The UK Patent Office (www.patent.gov.uk) has comprehensive information on intellectual property and is a good place to start, while the World Intellectual Property Organization (www.wipo.int) covers the international issues in more detail.

## Patents

Patent law is an old, established, complex and specialised area. In looking to protect your product with a patent, you'll need to take great care over the geographical range of protection the patent offers.

Obviously, global patent protection is much more costly than, say, the protection offered by a UK patent, but if you're thinking of marketing your invention abroad, it's important to have. There are several ways to proceed here. The UK is one of over 100 countries party to the Patent Cooperation Treaty, which allows you to file a single international patent application covering all the other countries that have signed the treaty. You can apply for this through the UK Patent Office, or with the World Intellectual Property Organization's International Bureau. The UK Patent Office website and WIPO websites both have information on the process.

But this is only the beginning. All applications for patents are renowned for being both lengthy and expensive, and due to certain difficulties – such as competition law imposing restrictions on the existence of monopolies – a patent may not always mean the holder has exclusive rights over its use. The UK Patent Office publishes the *Manual of Patent Practice*, which is certainly worth a look, as it will help you understand the basic principles of patenting. You can download the manual free from their website.

## Copyright

Copyright, usually signified by a © on published work, provides the owner (usually the author or their publisher or employer) with control of the publication and copying of the material, along with the right to say the author must be acknowledged for the work. There is no registration process: copyright simply happens where a record of work is credited.

Articles, books, films, sound recordings and so on can be copyrighted for a finite number of years. At the moment, literary work such as poems and novels are protected for 70 years after the death of the author; different periods and rules apply for other media.

Within the copyrighted period, permission must be sought from the owner, who may charge for reproducing the material or only ask for an acknowledgement. An infringement can mean big monetary penalties and even up to six months in jail. So where there is any concern about abuse of someone else's copyright, it is always wise to seek clarification from the author or owner.

## Non-disclosure agreements

Non-disclosure agreements (NDAs) or confidentiality agreements protect trade secrets from exposure. To ensure all parties are made aware of this right, a clause in your employment and service contracts can be a potential catch-all.

## Trademarks

Trademarks may require international protection and if you are a global business, you need to ensure international registration. Two treaties, the Madrid Agreement and the Madrid Protocol, cover 60 countries and are administered by WIPO. Check them (www.wipo.int/madrid/en/) to make sure you are covered for all your trading countries.

If you want to register your trademark, you'll need to contact the Trade Mark Registry, which is part of the UK Patent Office. The office publishes a useful manual on applying to register, downloadable free from their website.

It is worth noting that this can be a lengthy process, as the application must be published in the *Trade Marks Journal*, and three months must pass without anyone opposing it before registration can continue. However, this can be well worth the wait: trademarks are the only form of IP protection that last indefinitely – as long as you pay the 10-yearly fees!

## Designs

You can also protect a design by registering it in the UK through the Patent Office's Designs Registry. There is a useful publication on the process downloadable free from their website.

Your design must fulfil their criteria, however, which include being new and appealing to the eye of the consumer. Designs which are unregistered sometimes attract protection provided they are unique, but in these cases the length and extent of protection is less. So if the design is important enough to your business to warrant the cost, registration may be preferable. Take care, though, that you don't publicise your design before obtaining registration, as this in itself could scupper your chances and lead to refusal! The Patent Office keeps information regarding judgement on cases.

# Goodwill

Finally, there is the goodwill of your business – that is, anything that distinguishes it from its competitors and provides its identity and reputation. This can cover a number of forms of IP, such as trademarks and the name of your company. The extent to which goodwill can be protected is limited, however, to the geographical area in which it is well known.

As a result, you need to be careful not to choose marketing strategies, merchandising, trade names or anything else which is overly similar to a competitor's. Otherwise you may be seen as trying to confuse the consumer and 'pass off'[*1] your own business as connected to theirs, and so work off their goodwill and reputation in the market. Again, if in doubt, it is always better to investigate whether or not an abuse has taken place, as the cost can be high.

Whatever the form of your IP, irretrievable damage frequently happens via plagiarism or breaches, where the only recourse is litigation. However, that is not to say you shouldn't protect your IP. Just don't think of that protection as a panacea!

[*1] See Compliance, section 18, p. 109

# 10. Letterheads

If that be law, I'll go home and burn my books.
**Lord Mansfield**

My Lord, you'd better go home and read them.
**Lord Ashburton**

Thinking about a letterhead for your business can be a pleasure, as it's one of the ways you will present your creation to the world. So when you ponder possible designs, branding and image may be looming larger in your mind than any particular compliance requirements. But be aware that certain concerns take a front seat here, and they go deeper than mere appearance.

As well as clearly displaying your company's name – and don't forget that that may not be the same as your trading name – you must also put either your registered office address (which, again, may not be the same as your trading address) or your company number, which is available from Companies House. This measure means you can be properly traced for any official requirements.

If you list the names of directors, you must list *all* names, including those of shadow directors! So it's probably best to list none at all.

Make sure you are compliant with these conditions, as breaches are considered to be breaking the law.

# 11. Objects clause – *ultra vires*

> You cannot escape the responsibility of tomorrow by evading it today.
> **Abraham Lincoln**

When was the last time you looked at your Memorandum and Articles of Association? Be honest, now ... it might well have been a while ago. But as these are the documents that form the constitution of your business, and tell you what and how you can carry out business functions, it's important to know what is in them.

It is unfortunate that these texts are written in legal jargon, which doesn't exactly make them fun reading on a Friday night over a glass or two of Chablis. It's better to tackle them in the mornings – and towards the start of the week, when you're in serious mode. They are, after all, hugely important regarding one element in particular!

## Defining the limits

This crucial element is the objects clause – the statement in the Memorandum that effectively details exactly what type of activity your company can engage in. The range of activity might be exceedingly wide or very restrictive; it depends on who drew up your Articles and when.

The most important issue here is that you will be subject to penalties if you fail to adhere to the objects clause, or any issues relating to changing it – which you'll want to do if you wish to broaden the scope of your activities.

But for the moment, let's imagine that your clause doesn't actually give you permission to carry out your current activities – that is, you've breached it and acted ultra vires (beyond your powers).

First off, you need to know the implications of the breach:

1. Third parties are protected; the validity of a contract will rarely be questioned on the grounds of capacity.

2. Shareholders, however, may bring proceedings to restrain an action. So theoretically, they could stop the company from trading in the area it wasn't supposed to!

3. As a director, if you do not observe the limitations in your objects clause, you may be **personally** liable for the consequences!

It doesn't look good. So what can you do?

Change the clause, of course. To do this, you'll need to pass a special resolution, which requires a 75 per cent vote by your shareholders. But it may not all be smooth sailing. What if they don't agree, or you don't control their votes? Moreover, a successful change still won't make any existing breaches legal.

So note: if your business was formed some time ago, your Memorandum and Articles could be out of date, and no longer tally with your current trading profile.

Check it out and get it changed – **NOW!**

# 12. Partnership agreements

> The great thought, the great concern, the great anxiety of men is to restrict, as much as possible, the limits of their own responsibility.
> **Giosué Borsi, *A Soldier's Confidences with God***

A partnership is simply two or more people coming together with a view to making a profit. Under the Partnership Act, you need very little more.

This seems informal, and it is – not least in the implications for liability. Each of the partners is responsible for all of the liabilities of the partnership – in other words, any debts incurred in the name of the partnership are the responsibility of all the partners, and if they're not covered by partnership funds, the partners will have to dig into their own personal assets to pay them off.

Clearly, an agreement with this level of informality can be fraught with potential problems, and as a partner is liable for the acts of his fellow partners, some sort of structure would seem sensible. Just like shareholder agreements,[*1] a partnership agreement is something that should be sorted out and agreed when all parties are getting on so well they don't think they need one – **not** when a dispute occurs.

## How to get it right

A partnership agreement is essentially a binding document that outlines the agreement between the parties stating what they are allowed and expected to do and receive in the name of the partnership. It will also cover such issues as cessation – that is, what happens when a partner dies, or falls out with the others. And it should discuss profit allocation and rules related to decision-making – such as who has the right to decide on capital expenditure limits and plans, senior staff recruitment or customer and supplier management issues.

You need to describe your agreement as fully as possible. Implied agreements are much more difficult to prove and demonstrate if any acrimonious situations arise in your partnership.

Just as with a shareholders' agreement, a partnership agreement is not always in the public domain, and it only binds those who sign it.

In any case, because personal liabilities figure so large in these agreements, why have further issues to worry about such as who is allowed to do what, why and when, when this can all be dealt with in a properly constructed document!

If you do not have a partnership agreement, the Partnership Act

[*2] See Structure, section 18, p. 39

will imply that all the partners share profits equally and own the partnership business equally. In such a case exiting the partnership is also more difficult (both for the retiring partner and those left behind) and more likely to involve expensive legal disputes. You will not have any restrictive covenants either, so the retiring partner can set up in competition.

Remember that partners who share in the profits are not employees, so employment legislation does not apply to them.

Tax treatment of partners is complex: you'll need advice on this one.

You may see reference to a 'salaried partner' – someone who is paid a salary but shown as a partner on the notepaper (usually as a matter of status). A salaried partner will not generally share in the profits (or losses), may be an employee, and will either have no role in management or a limited role. This is a dangerous position for the salaried partner, as he or she is liable to creditors but gets none of the benefits of sharing in profits!

One case I recall involved a litigious action against a partnership which included four equity partners and one salaried partner. The salaried partner, who was much wealthier than his colleagues, was very upset indeed to discover that when an action was brought against the partnership, joint and several liability*2 meant he had to provide considerably more funds to the pursuing (and in this case successful) creditors.

*2 See Funding, section 11, p. 67

# 13. Phantom share schemes

October. This is one of the peculiarly dangerous
months to speculate in stocks. The others are July,
January, September, April, November, May, March,
June, December, August and February.
**Mark Twain**

Let's say you would like to give your staff an incentive by offering
them a chance to participate in the increasing value of the business as a whole, but you don't want to – or perhaps can't –
provide for a scheme that gives them access to actual shares.

The alternative is to set up a phantom share scheme. Like most
things, such schemes have positive and negative elements.

First, though, what are phantom shares? This is the technical
name given to hypothetical shares of a company's common
stock, based on the market value of the stock at a given time. A
phantom share scheme basically allows staff (any, all or just
specific ones) an incentive based on building corporate value
rather than, say, just profits or sales performance (although
clearly there is a link to these in terms of company worth).

The scheme can be set up quite informally, but it's best to take
legal advice to avoid any confusion arising at a later stage.

The scheme could be linked to the increase in perceived value as
determined by an agreed valuation method, for instance, or by a
valuation completed by a third party. For example, you could say
that an employee would be designated 10 per cent phantom
shares in your business once a valuation of a given amount was
achieved, or even that they would just acquire that percentage
when you sell the company allowing them to have a share in the
proceeds of the sale.

The downside for the employee is that this gain will be treated
as income rather than a capital gain. So their tax charge could be
as much as 40 per cent if they are a higher-rate tax payer.

## The upsides

If that is a downside, however, there are lots of upsides – provided you have closed any legal loopholes.

If your employee leaves, they don't take their phantom shares with them, so you need no shareholder agreement and you needn't worry about dividend payments. Equally, they have no say in the running of the company, as they don't officially have any ownership of it.

As you can see, this is a lot less cumbersome than a formal structured share scheme. The fact that it is less visible than such a scheme may prove less of an incentive for your management, but it is better than nothing (if nothing is the only alternative).

Don't do what one client did, however. They failed to make it absolutely clear that this benefit was only available if the individual concerned was still in employment. When the employee left under less than agreeable circumstances, my client found he had a 'breach of contract' problem to deal with on top of the employment tribunal!

# 14. PLC non listed

> The rung of a ladder was never meant to rest upon, but only to hold a man's foot long enough to enable him to put the other somewhat higher.
> **Thomas Henry Huxley, *Life and Letters of Thomas Huxley***

The initials PLC after a company name stand, of course, for 'public limited company'. You might think that this means the business must be listed on a stock exchange of some sort. But you'd be wrong – partly at least.

PLC can and does mean that the business trades on the London

Stock Exchange (LSE) or the Alternative Investment Market (AIM) or even on Ofex, the third small market, which isn't part of the LSE. But did you know you can also call your company PLC and not actually be a listed business?

Of course, certain conditions apply. For instance, you must have a minimum of £50,000 of share capital (although only 25 per cent needs to be paid up, so in theory you could have a PLC company with only £12,500 of paid-up capital).

Please be aware, however, that if your company goes into liquidation, the shareholders would have to provide the unpaid balance of share capital.

In addition, instead of the requirement for one director and one shareholder that is the standard for limited companies (Ltd), you will need two directors – of whom one could also take up the company secretary role – plus two shareholders.

## Feeling the squeeze

Your deadlines for filing accounts at Companies House are also shorter than for a limited company. Instead of the 10-month requirement, you will only have seven months from your year end. At the same time, your potential audit costs may be a little higher than for a limited company.

A PLC is also required to have a qualified company secretary.

So why bother? Usually, it's for the kudos. First impressions are hugely important, and when you hand out a business card or write to someone on a letterhead with PLC instead of Ltd after your company's name, there is a general assumption that it has substance.

# 15. Restraint of trade/restrictive covenants

You're only as good as the people you hire.
**Ray Kroc, founder of the McDonalds Corporation**

A restrictive covenant is effectively an agreement to try to restrict an employee's actions after he has left your employment. They are usually entered into service*[1] or employment contracts*[2] where it is believed they are necessary to protect the employers 'legitimate business interests'.

Restrictive covenants are intended to protect the business – not to penalise a director who wishes to leave. So you need to make sure that the covenants are just restrictive enough to secure the company's business. If you get it wrong, the covenant may fail completely.

## Enforceability issues

The enforceability of such a clause is, of course, critical, and several issues need to be considered in relation to it:

1. Can the restriction be reasonably expected to protect the interests of the business (and it is for the employer to prove this, not for the ex-employee to prove it isn't!)?

2. To be reasonable, consideration will include both time limits and geographical location.

3. To prove the legitimacy of the business interest, the employer will have to prove they have some 'proprietary right' over the matters being protected. Traditionally these have included trade secrets, details of customers, suppliers and so forth.

*[1] See Structure, section 8, p. 18
*[2] See Compliance, section 2, p. 85

These need to be specified, since a general duty is much more difficult to enforce.

It should not be thought, however, that putting in place restrictions on future competition or confidentiality will solve all your problems if a key director leaves.

Enforceability depends on getting evidence (sometimes from customers who have decided to deal with the 'deserter'), so part of your corporate governance risk strategy should look at how to protect your company's business, contacts and secrets in such a way that one exiting director can't severely damage the business.

In reviewing the contract, many issues will be taken into account in relation to the confidentiality clause. This will include what sort of job the employee worked in, what their specific role was, whether they had access to privileged information, and whether any of that information is now in the public domain. None of these issues will necessarily be conclusive in its own right, but they will be considered as a whole in relation to a judgment.

The non-solicitation clause, which if enforceable would prevent an employee from poaching colleagues, suppliers or customers, may be acceptable for some classes of employees. For example, a sales manager may be prevented for a reasonable period from approaching his customers, but may not be excluded from approaching a colleague to come and work with him at his new place of employment.

No clause will be acceptable if it prevents the person who is leaving from earning a living. Indeed, you should note that the courts will not rewrite a covenant to make it acceptable – they will merely delete it. So great care and advice must be taken in drafting those clauses.

One clause I recall as being thrown out of court was a restriction on an operations director who was leaving to relocate elsewhere in the country for personal reasons. The clause sought to stop him from taking up any job in the sector in the UK for 12 months. Once it was rejected, the director in question immediately went to work for the competition!

Equally, if an employee brings a successful claim for wrongful dismissal or breach of contract, they will not be bound by any restrictive covenants. Paying an employee a sum in lieu of notice can, in the absence of a specific claim authorising this, amount to a breach of contract.

# 16. Role of the company secretary

A human being must have occupation if he or she is not to become a nuisance to the world.
**Dorothy L. Sayers, British author and Christian Humanist**

Every company is legally obliged to appoint a company secretary. This person need not be a director of the company, but will become an officer.

The role includes a substantial amount of legal responsibilities, and should never be taken on lightly. In smaller businesses most of the work is to do with ensuring the company is complying with the relevant laws and regulations, but there are around 150 offences that you can be made personally accountable for if you do not adhere to the requirements.

In a private company there is no requirement for the role to be held by a professionally qualified person, although this is not the case in a PLC. As your company gets more substantial, the technical requirements may become more onerous. In this case it is worth considering delegating the role of company secretary to a professional provider, such as your accountant (although not auditor) or lawyer, or there are any number of specialist firms who can supply you with the service, for which relatively modest fees are charged.

## The range of duties

Along with the filing of various annual returns, the company secretary is also responsible for monitoring and registering the company's registered office. This means ensuring that documents sent there can be dealt with and that shareholders who have the right to inspect them can access them when and if they so choose.

You are even responsible for ensuring your company is compliant in relation to corporate stationery – specifically letter-heads, which must carry the company's registered number and address and if a decision is taken to list any directors, all must be included, even shadow directors[1]. And you must maintain the statutory and legal books and records, and manage the information and changes to corporate and board structure with Companies House.

You will probably be arranging the board meeting process, including taking and keeping minutes along with arranging the AGMs and EGMs as needed.

Although the principal legal requirements will rest with the board of directors, the company secretary can be held jointly liable. A breach of the law could involve fines or even imprisonment as punishment.

The Institute of Chartered Secretaries and Administrators (ICSA) runs training courses for company secretaries, and Companies House can also provide you with relevant booklets to help keep you up to date.

Do not, as so many clients have done, appoint 'the wife' simply as a means of providing her with remuneration – you also give her a whole lot of liability she would rather not have!

[1] See Structure, section 10, p. 25

# 17. Shadow directors

I am rather like a mosquito in a nudist camp; I know
what I ought to do, but I don't know where to begin.
**Stephen Bayne, Executive Officer, Anglican Communion**

Directors of companies **do not** have limited liabilities – companies have limited liabilities. That means that in the case of liquidation, it's possible for the liquidator to bring actions against **you personally** in the form of a contribution order. This would force you to contribute to any creditor shortfall, if you haven't acted in an appropriate manner and the liquidator is able to prove this.

So it is essential to identify just who is and isn't a director.

You become a formally appointed director when your 288a form is received at Companies House. Companies House lists all registered directors and it is possible to search them by name (www.companieshouse.co.uk).

## Out of the shadows

But what if you think you aren't a director – or are convinced you aren't, as you have not submitted any form to Companies House? The problem is that you can be a director without intent or knowledge (see 'Appointment, remuneration and removal of directors', starting on page 8). Such people are called shadow directors and are indeed defined as such in the Companies Act.

Essentially, in layman's terms, a shadow director is someone who acts like a director and makes decisions like a director, who the other directors look to for guidance and advice, and whose advice they indeed follow.

Generally, the professionals – that is, your auditor, lawyer and so on – are excluded from being shadow directors as long as they stay within the remit of their engagement and just provide advice rather than give directions or instructions, although there have been a couple of high-profile examples where they have not escaped liability.

In the case of **RBS v Bacon**, the Royal Bank of Scotland found themselves in the position of being shadow directors due to their excessive involvement in Mr Bacon's company, and in a more recent case a firm of chartered accountants became increasingly involved in the day-to-day running of a company in distress, only to find when the company eventually folded that they were regarded as part of the board.

The unfortunate thing for shadow directors is that they may not know they have taken up this position, and indeed the officially appointed members of the board might have had no intention of putting them into that role. Rather, it is their actions and the relationship with the board which have in fact created the situation.

A case I recall went as follows (names have been changed to protect the innocent!).

Mr Hardup was the sole owner/director of his company, which found itself in decline. Being somewhat incompetent in money matters, Mr Hardup had continued to order goods and services which he was unable to pay for. Eventually, the business folded.

Mr Hardup ran the company with considerable involvement from his bookkeeper. This man was not an appointed director, but he largely managed the finances on a day-to-day basis and gave Mr Hardup regular instruction on financial management.

When the liquidator decided to bring an action against the directors to ask them for a contribution towards the shortfall faced by the creditors, Mr Hardup's bookkeeper found himself in the unfortunate position of being classed as a director, and having to contribute to the creditors' 'pot'.

Senior personnel are clearly most at risk, and it would be fair to say they are particularly so in a smaller company.

How can you protect them? Ensure that senior personnel report to the board and give advice; but also ensure that the board make their own decisions and ratify the actions of senior management teams. Also recommend that the board take minutes detailing such decisions, so there is evidence that the decisions were made solely by those charged with such responsibility – that is, the directors.

The motto for directors is: delegate, don't abdicate!

# 18. Shareholders' agreements

Jesus picked up twelve men from the bottom ranks of business and forged them into an organisation that conquered the world.
**Bruce Barton, American advertising guru**

Two men I know had a great company. It had been established for years and made them both a lot of money. It had a prestigious market position and was a substantial employer in the region. The company was jointly owned, 50/50, with only the two of them as directors.

Sounds very cosy, and indeed it was. In fact, it worked very, very well until, like many 'marriages', the two men developed irreconcilable differences.

Of course, these things happen. People fall out, change, or simply want different things out of life. However, in business it's important to look at such a potential breakdown dispassionately – so any shareholder in a private company should consider what will happen if the unthinkable occurs.

## Preparing for the worst

In all private companies, shareholders should have some sort of agreement on how to deal with issues surrounding the sale and disposal of their shareholding, what happens on the death of a shareholder and disagreements over share transfers.

In the particular case discussed above, the absence of any form of agreement cost the company, and the two individuals concerned, several hundred thousand pounds to resolve. The money all went to pay the fees of legal and corporate financiers negotiating on their behalf for a deal. If a shareholder agreement had existed, of course, all that would have been unnecessary.

Here are a few key issues to think about:

1. The courts generally will not intervene to resolve shareholder disputes.

    In the case above, one party fell out with the other and was determined to buy his fellow partner out. After a great deal of very expensive discussion, it was finally agreed that a sale would go ahead. The next and critical problem was, of course, at what value.

    In the meantime, the value of the business was deteriorating, as neither could dismiss the other or hire/dismiss other staff. Relationships with employees, customers and suppliers alike began falling by the wayside. And as both shareholders were cheque signatories, there was complete intransigence. Indeed, if one decided not to come to work due to stress he would of course still have to be paid! (So what value is a private company? The bottom line is essentially what one party will sell at and the other buy at.)

    After even more money and time – lots of time, in fact almost 12 months of it – a very inequitable deal was struck. Inequitable, that is, for the buyer, who paid a very substantial premium, simply to get the deal done!

2. If you die, your shares pass on to your estate – and quite rightly so ... unless, of course, the beneficiaries are not exactly ideal bedfellows for the other shareholders, such as children, nonworking spouses, charities and so on, who have an entirely different agenda from executive shareholders.

    To deal with this, it is essential that pre-emption rights and cross-option arrangements are written into the agreement. These essentially give incumbent shareholders both the legal rights and – provided the scheme is backed by an insurance policy on the life of the shareholder for the benefit of the other shareholder(s) – the wherewithal to acquire the shares, so that the estate is not penalised and the organisation retains control.

3. Share valuation is **always** an issue.

As any dispute almost always relates to the value of shares, some sort of valuation mechanism is essential, with an arbitration clause as a mandatory requirement. This alone will save thousands of pounds and weeks, if not months, of discussion, so keep it up to date! Be wary of using the auditor as a valuer. One recent case highlighted the fact that the exiting shareholder felt the auditors were simply too close to the remaining shareholder to be truly impartial.

4. Sort out deadlock clauses.

It is only being realistic to accept that there may well be occasions where 50 per cent of your shareholders hold a different view from the other 50 per cent. For instance, half your shareholders may wish to accept an offer for the sale of the whole of the company, while the other half are emphatically against the idea. This inevitably creates a stalemate, along with some pretty frustrated owners who can't 'get their own way'.

If it's generally felt within the company that this could happen at some stage, you'll need to sort out how to manage the situation. This is where deadlock clauses come in. These can take the form of an undertaking that if the parties don't agree, they will take part in a procedure to come to terms. This could be binding or not: for instance, it could call for the use of a professional mediator to sort out the deadlock, or for both parties to attend a formal arbitration hearing and agree to be bound by the findings.

5. Anyone controlling 10 per cent of the shares or more does not have to follow the other 90 per cent unless special provisions apply.

   Imagine you are offered the deal of your dreams. The price offered for your company exceeds your wildest expectations, but you only control 80 per cent of the shares. Your buyer wants the whole business, but your fellow shareholders don't want to go along with your idea – end of dream!

   To manage this sort of situation, you need to have a 'drag along' clause. This is a clause that forces the minority to follow the majority, set at whatever level the parties agree would resolve this problem. To preserve fairness, the majority may also agree that if they wish to sell a controlling interest to a third party, they will do so only if they first ensure that the minority can sell on the same terms. This is called a 'tag along' clause.

6. The shareholders' agreement, unlike the Memorandum and Articles of Association, only binds those partners who sign it … so it **must** be kept up to date following any transfer of shares.

Most people don't get married with the intention of divorcing in the future, and most shareholders in private companies don't think about later disputes. But inevitably, there will be issues at a later date and time, so sort the shareholders' agreement out during the courtship, not in the divorce courts. In other words, ensure these matters are agreed upon at the start of the relationship; keep the agreement up to date; and get good advice as soon as possible.

# 19. Statement of reserved powers

If everyone is thinking alike then somebody isn't thinking.
**George S. Patton, US General**

The authority of your directors comes in both implied and authorised form. Their authorised authority might be detailed in their job description or even in appointment documents. Their implied authority, however, is a whole different ball game.

Take you board quorum.[1] As you may remember, most private companies tend to have a default quorum of two. If so, two of your directors could call a board meeting. This would require 'reasonable' notice, but that is not defined in terms of length of time; and if no other directors attended, they could make decisions without recourse to the whole board. Not good – particularly if they make a commitment that will bind you, the rest of the board and your company.

Now clearly, it is neither sensible nor reasonable to ask directors to defer every decision to the whole board. But crucial decisions are another thing altogether. Do you really want one of your directors talking to the press about a major crisis (for example) without reference to the board?

## Taking the measure of power

In order to manage this process it is very valuable indeed to outline in detail the actual authority levels that individuals or groups of individual directors have in your business. This will ensure a degree of accountability. And one method of ensuring good practice in this regard is to create a statement of reserved powers.

[1] See Structure, section 4, p. 10

This is a document adopted by the board which expressly states those areas that must be brought to the board for validation, and further discussion if needed, before a decision can be taken.

The length and depth of this document depends on the business in question, but could contain, for example:
- Approval of capital expenditure over a certain limit
- Changes in the business management structure
- Substantial acquisitions
- Press release approvals
- And whatever else is deemed appropriate.

Bearing in mind the potential liability each director has for each other, it makes very good sense indeed to ensure that your whole board is involved in critical decision-making.

If your company is small and all the directors are shareholders, levels of authority could be interpolated into the shareholders' agreement[1].


# 20. Unlimited companies

Do what you can, with what you have, where you are.
**Theodore Roosevelt**


An unlimited company seems a bit of an oxymoron. However, they do exist as a corporate structure option, although the business world is hardly swarming with them.

In the more usual limited liability company, the liability of the shareholders is limited to the amount of funds they have invested in the business via the share capital account. Unlimited companies, however, have one significant difference.

For the shareholders or members of these types of companies

[1] See Structure, section 18, p. 39

(like partners in a partnership), there are no limits on their personal contribution to a shortfall in funds, should the business fail.

Why on earth, then, would anyone want such a corporate vehicle?

As such entities are companies in all but the above sense, they have certain advantages that shareholders may value, particularly from the taxation point of view. These include the ability to hold and own property via a corporate body, and provide debentures.[1] So they are classed as registered companies and taxed in the same way as any other type of company owned by shareholders. But of most interest to some owners is that there is no requirement to file accounts in the public domain for such a company, so confidentiality about the company's performance, assets and liabilities can be maintained. Some shareholders may feel that this advantage outweighs the unlimited liability aspect.

The only specific requirement is that there must be a minimum of two shareholders and two directors (normal limited companies only need one).

[1] See Funding, section 9, p. 63

# Funding: the ins and outs of raising money

Remind people that profit is the difference between revenue and expense. This makes you look smart.
**Scott Adams, creator of the Dilbert comic strip**

'Money makes the world go around', according to the song in *Cabaret*. And so it does – the business world, at any rate. You simply can't run a business without some working capital.

Cash is vital. You can trade indefinitely at a loss, but you cannot trade without cash, and they are not the same (never forget that!).

Although you might not think it, there is money available to fund your business – lots of it! However, that is not to say:

1. You will be able to find it

2. You will want it (on the terms offered, anyway).

What is very important is to ensure you borrow the right kind and amount of money in the first place. Most people wildly underestimate what they actually need. Costs are always more than you think, transactions take longer to come to fruition than you might have planned, and matters are never instantaneously corrected (unless you are very fortunate). So you need to build contingencies into your plans.

## Matching need to fund

The most important part of funding is to match the need to the fund. You may in any case encounter problems sourcing the money in the first place, but a big mismatch means even more of a problem when the money has to be redeemed.

This is because credit committees in banks are interested in security and the borrower's ability to service the debt. So if you borrow on an overdraft for what is effectively a capital spend, they have a different view of the security and interest needed than if they can take security against the capital item being purchased.

The banking profession is usually very cautious indeed. They want security (and lots of it), and they want to be convinced that you can service the debt. They are inundated with potential deals, so make sure your proposition stands out. Be optimistically realistic and don't forget your contingencies: it's painfully embarrassing and sometimes impossible to go back for a second helping if you didn't originally anticipate the need for it!

Although we do like to follow American practice in certain circumstances, and although there is a softening in the law in relation to bankruptcy and directors, the English belief that in all probability one failure means another is still prevalent. So you cannot afford to get it wrong, as this is likely to prejudice your case for funding a second time round.

Interest costs have been low of late, so provided you have a sound business case it is generally good for businesses to borrow money – provided, of course, that you can make more than it's costing you! But you must maximise funds within your own business.

Manage your debt collection, take advantage of settlement allowances and raise capital personally wherever it's applicable. Usually you can do this at better rates and over longer periods than the business itself, and if you have to provide a personal guarantee against a business debt in any case, a director's loan may actually be better for you, as it will allow you to spread the debt.

## Investment agreements

Look very, very carefully at investment agreements. They can be terrifyingly long, and are often written in complex and confusing legal jargon which you'll probably have difficulty deciphering. Negotiate long and hard at the start: it is almost impossible to change terms in your favour at a later stage.

Check the small print and if you are in any way confused, keep asking for clarification until you are perfectly clear.

The right type of funding will take longer to put in place than the wrong type. But be assured that this is time well spent that could save you substantial heartache if things go wrong at a later stage.

Finally, keep a tight grip on your funding to try to anticipate well in advance any changes you may need to make. Keep your funding bodies will informed. You'll then find when you need to turn to them they will be a lot more receptive. Treat them as a partner, but don't forget they are a supplier!

# 1. Angels

Most people like hard work. Particularly when they are paying for it.
**Franklin P. Jones, US businessman and founder of the American Management Association**

Aside from the winged variety, people who invest amounts with a high net worth into a business are known as angels. These people, who sometimes operate on their own or in structured groups such as the National Business Angels Network, are a very useful and valuable source of funding for smaller transactions that require some equity from a third party.

Accessing hundreds of thousands of pounds of equity from conventional sources is very difficult, but if you find the right angel, they can provide amounts from as little as £10,000 up to £1,000,000 or more, with syndication.

Like investment opportunities, angels are a variable lot. Some will want to take a very proactive role in the business, though more often than not their investment is very passive, involving little more than perhaps a seat as a non-executive on your board.

## Proactive or passive?

Each type of investment has a different appeal. If you are short on management, a proactive angel may be a godsend. However, make sure that your growth and management ideas match your investor's, as they will end up being much more than an employee.

> I had one case where a very enthusiastic angel invested in a concern making 'kit cars' solely to indulge his personal passion in the product. It was an unsuccessful relationship for both parties because it wasn't based on business reasons – that is, profit, company growth and the like – but instead, on the investor's personal interests. As a result, this angel was unable to take a hardnosed decision related to finance at a crucial moment, and the enterprise failed.

If your management is in good shape, a 'hands-off' angel may be more to your taste.

Angels often invest via ordinary shares, mostly to allow them maximum tax relief. And clearly, this has a lot of advantages for the investment company, as ordinary shares only result in a dividend if all other ordinary shareholders get one.

Angel organisations exist all over the country. There are even international groups, which may well be worth contacting depending on your product.

Angel deals are happening everywhere, but it's vital to note that they are 'slow boil'. In other words, it often takes a very long time to bring them to fruition, so don't expect a quick fix.

Exit requirements can also be very variable. Some people are happy to 'sit' on their investment, sometimes fairly indefinitely, particularly if the company is doing well and dividend flow is good. Others encourage the management towards a speedy exit via floats and trade sales. So ensure you discuss the 'out' as well as the 'in' with your angel, to ensure all parties have the same objectives.

Also don't forget the shareholders' agreement,[*1] and get your pre-emption clauses into a satisfactory state from the start of the investment.

# 2. Bank discounting projections

If you spend money on it, it's a hobby; if you make money on it, it's a business.
**Sally Rand, famous fan dancer and star of Chicago World's Fair**

If you run a business you will run up against the need to borrow money. And to do that you'll need to impress the bank or some other funder. But bank funders are, by and large, a fairly cautious bunch. Even if they say they will take a risk, this is usually a very measured one indeed.

So if they ask for some financial projections, this isn't an unreasonable requirement. After all, the funders want to make sure you can make the repayment schedule with ease.

Here are a few inside tips:

1. Your operating profit must be a minimum of three times the interest payable to give any degree of comfort.

---

[*1] See Structure, section 18, p. 39

2.  Submit some best-case and worst-case scenarios, but with the worst cases be very wary that they do not drop below the bank's thresholds on lending criteria, such as the one above. Otherwise, you will discount yourself out of the facility! Remember: banks have a tendency to look coldly at numbers. Two plus two will always be four, even if we want it to be five.

3.  Banks will discount your estimate by as much as 20 per cent, so take this into account in your projections.

4.  Don't exaggerate your various scenarios so much that they are totally unrealistic. Banks want information to be as reliable and accurate as possible, and are highly sceptical of 'hockey stick' projections.

5.  Equally, submitting projections so low that they are easily beaten won't do you any favours, as the banks will have no confidence in your ability to forecast accurately.

It's very simple: banks want security for the debt and an ability to finance the interest and repay the loans on time. They need to feel secure that you can achieve this now and in the future, as otherwise their recourse will be to seize the asset via an insolvency procedure or call in a guarantee,[*1] which could be yours!

---

[*1] See Funding, section 14, p. 72

# 3. BVCA minimum/maximum investment

A 35-year-old corporate finance adviser died of a heart attack and challenged St Peter: 'Why now?' 'Well,' said St Peter, 'we looked at the bills you have sent your clients and reckoned you must have been at least 90 to have charged that many billable hours.'
**From the Chartered Institute of Taxation website**

If you are thinking about a possible equity investor and don't want to talk to your professional advisers just yet (although I urge you to do this sooner rather than later!), the British Venture Capital Association (BVCA) is as good a place as any to start an investigation process.

Founded in 1983, the BVCA represents the vast majority of private equity and venture capital in the UK. They have an excellent website (www.bvca.co.uk) and lots of free publications.

You can contact them online, which will allow you to input critical data, including industry type, location, type of investment and so on. Their search engine then identifies possible investors. When you analyse these, one particular field will tell you the funder's minimum and maximum investment criteria – a useful pointer in its own right.

However, caution is needed. Smaller equity investments are notoriously difficult to secure. (Generally speaking, smaller means less than a million.)

Of course, there are some funders who will provide these more conservative levels of funds; but they tend to be regional investors or specialist industry players. So use the minimum figure with a degree of caution.

As for start-up funding, although a number of BVCA members say they will look at this kind of transaction, in reality such bodies are few and far between. Start-up funding based on third party equity is virtually impossible to secure.

Of course, this doesn't completely rule such deals out; but as many come through non-mainstream funders, they may not necessarily be members of the BVCA. They could be angels or even other commercial companies looking for a joint venture.

Access may be better identified through your professional advisers, who often have sector knowledge and contacts that can circumvent problems.

Here's an inside tip: a good corporate financier will have personal contacts with lots of these funding providers. In the first stage this can at the very least get your proposition looked at seriously. And considering the number of enquiries these organisations get, that's quite an achievement.

# 4. Contingent fees and due diligence costs

Time is money.
**Benjamin Franklin,** *Advice to a Young Tradesman*

'No win, no fee.' These days, every other commercial seems to indoctrinate you into the philosophy of success-based litigation or service provision.

For instance, it is now commonplace for corporate financiers and indeed corporate lawyers to provide a management buy-out (MBO) team with a contingent fee proposal – that is, a fee paid only if the buy-out is successful. Thus ensuring you do not have to be concerned about the payment of expensive professional fees if the deal fails.

Unless a transaction is a very modest one, you will almost certainly need advice on structuring the deal, raising finance and legal compliance. So if you can negotiate a situation where fees for this advice are only payable if the deal completes – that is, no win, no fee – then you have no financial risk.

But the downside can be serious. Professionals have to earn a living! (I can just hear you saying 'Ahhhh'!) And as such if a deal does not come to fruition, very often extensive amounts of time simply have to be written off. In order to compensate for this, expect to have to pay a premium on recorded time. This can be any percentage, dependent on the risk perceived by the advisers – as little as 30 per cent and as much as 200 per cent – and frankly is usually negotiable.

You may be able to temper this outcome if, for instance, the vendor was willing to underwrite some or all of the fees – not an unusual practice in a friendly MBO, but certainly not a given. And it may give rise to financial assistance issues.[1]

You do need to negotiate hard, though, if the deal does go through. Fees are usually taken at completion, and almost always need to be raised along with vendor consideration and working capital requirements – that is, the money paid to the vendor for the value of their company, and the money needed to run the company on a day-to-day basis.

## All about due diligence

Even if it is possible to negotiate in this area, costs and payment terms may be less malleable for an important process related to MBOs: due diligence.

Due diligence is basically an appraisal of an acquisition – an investigation into the company's affairs to validate the lender's decision, or the commercial decision to buy in the first place. A funder, for instance, may set up a due diligence exercise to check the financial robustness of the acquisition targeted in an MBO. It is prepared on behalf of the funder by a third party, but payable by the buyer's company. However, if the deal aborts for whatever reason, **you** – the MBO team – will be asked to underwrite these fees in most cases.

[1] See Exiting, section 3, p. 189

The reason is clear. If these fees were contingent, there would be unacceptable pressure on the due diligence team to write a favourable report – not exactly what the funder might want, unless of course it is all positive!

These fees can frankly be for any amount. It all depends on the deal size, type of transaction and the due diligence provider.

What you should be seeking to do is minimise exposure by allowing your corporate financier to negotiate the best deal with the funders in relation to the due diligence provider and the terms of reference. That is part of their job – let them help you!

A recent quote on due diligence investigations offered to three different parties brought in proposals for £12,000, £8,000 and £5,000 – even though the funders specified exactly the same scope for all of them!

# 5. Credit approval

Always live within your income, even if you have to borrow money to do so.
**Josh Billings, pen name of humorist born Henry Wheeler Shaw, 1818**

Your bank managers can be some of the most vital friends you'll ever make. Get to know them – and at the same time, get them to understand and believe in your business. Hound them – if you get on with them, stay with them even when they relocate to a new branch. After all, the relationship you have with them is more important than the one you've got with the bank or branch. My own bankers are based 100 miles plus from my home!

Get to know what their lending powers are without recourse to credit approval – that is, an opinion on risk and an approval (or disapproval) given by a designated panel of people. Your manager won't divulge their own lending powers readily, but keep on trying in any case. This information is hugely important if you have built up a satisfactory relationship with your bank manager. For instance, when you need to extend your facilities for whatever reason, you want him to authorise this if at all possible without recourse to the movers and shakers at another level.

But sometimes, this clearly won't be possible. Either your manager hasn't got the level of authority necessary to meet your debt requirement, or – because of a variety of circumstances – referral to credit has got to happen. An example would be if your business is looking for rescue finance and your manager needs the security personally of a second opinion.

## Tipping the balance

In these cases, credit approval comes into play. And while the panels who do the job are meant to be independent, the truth is that they can be swayed considerably by the emphasis put on the proposal and the personal recommendations put forward by the proposing manager. That is not to say that a glowing report will necessarily guarantee success, but inevitably it does have some considerable degree of influence on a particular proposal.

With this in mind, remember that a deal is never done until it's done! Don't even think about cracking open the champagne until the funds are cleared into your account. Just because your bank manager says he will do the deal doesn't necessarily mean he can!

> Some banks (and I won't name them) have a nasty habit of promising too much, then not delivering. One bank, for instance, changed the covenants at the last minute when it was virtually too late to back out. So be warned.
>
> During one recent transaction, this same bank suddenly refused to lend unsecured sums promised to the MBO team for their investment. This delayed the deal by two months while we found another funder!

If possible, try to find out (with the help of your advisers if you need it) what the major requirements for credit approval are from your particular funder. And make sure you hit all the right buttons both in terms of how and when you make the presentation, as well as sensitivity testings on performance.

It is possible that if you are too cautious, for instance in a business plan, a sensitivity exercise will bring levels of performance down below an accepted waterline. Equally, overambitious projections will lose you credibility.

Changing requirements on a deal pitch may result in the need to revisit credit committees – not a route to be recommended, as once again this will test your credibility in terms of your understanding of the need in the first place. So: always think contingencies early on in negotiations.

# 6. Default interest, right of set off and retention of title

Marriage is like a bank account. You put it in, you take it out, you lose interest.
**Irwin Corey, American comic and film actor**

A sale is not a sale, really and truly, until you have banked the money. You need to keep this in mind: credit management is a fairly vital part of many businesses.

Getting paid on time, or indeed getting paid at all, can sometimes be a nightmare. And it often causes the poor supplier to fail. There are, however, a few tools in your kit box that may be of some help.

## Default interest

The first is the use of default interest, a technique used often by the banking community to penalise errant borrowers. It allows a lender to charge a higher interest rate (usually very high indeed) if some covenant is broken, for instance a loan non-payment.

To be binding, however, the supplier or lender must make a positive statement of intent specifying the default rate percentage. Care needs to be taken regarding the extent of the rate itself, as substantial differences in the usual rate compared to the default rate have been rejected by the courts.

Also, default interest rates can be disallowed if you stop payments and then start again after a break, say on a loan with a set time for repayment.

## Right of set off

Another method of cash collection adopted by the banking community is to create a right of set off.

It's not unusual for a borrower to have several accounts with a lender, some in credit and some with funds owing. The right of set off, if involved, would allow the lender to meet outstanding payments by transferring sums from the account in the black to one in the red. Note that the accounts must all be held in the same capacity to allow this to happen; so you can't do this with a personal account and a business account, for instance.

There is no legal requirement to inform customers of debt transfer, although it would seem good practice to do so. Any or all of these circumstances can be modified by mutual agreement.

## Retention of title

A further remedy to attempt to secure funds is retention of title, sometimes known as a Romalpa clause after a famous case in 1976. A Romalpa clause essentially says that although the buyer may have possession of your goods, he has no ownership until the debt attached has been satisfied.

In order for the clause to be effective, a positive statement regarding this right must be made. Also, the buyer must in turn acknowledge and accept this condition of sale, preferably before he enters into the contract. So merely putting terms on the back of an invoice is unlikely to be sustainable, particularly in a 'one off' sale situation.

Tracking the actual goods is also critical, as the retention right belongs only to goods not paid for. This can become hugely problematic when your goods are processed and become part of another commodity, or have been sold to a third party. Because of this, it is advisable to have retention rights that provide for recovery from third parties of the proceeds of those sales.

You should also be aware that printed terms alone will not protect the parties; the court, in making a decision, will always take into account what they see was the true intention behind the terms, even if this contradicts what actually happened in the past. Consistency is therefore vital.

Getting the goods back, however, is quite a different matter. If the customer has become insolvent, for instance, any evidence of your retention rights will be beneficial to say the least, so let the liquidator know of these as soon as possible (even though they will invariably say it is not binding!). Watch out for administrators selling your goods at below market value: they still have to give you the true sale price and not the forced one if you have been able to prove your retention right.

So, to summarise retention of title:

1. Ensure your retention clause is part of your sale contract.

2. Make sure the buyer acknowledges and agrees to its existence, and where this isn't possible for whatever reason, ensure that it is clearly specified on all corporate material, such as brochures, delivery notes and quotes.

3. Ensure that you have a system that can track your products to the outstanding invoice or, better still, use an 'all monies' clause. This provides the title to any goods supplied by you for any outstanding account.

4. Attach a term that prevents your goods being used as security for anything else.

Finally, nothing beats dealing with someone who will pay you in the first place! So consider insurance or proforma (where customers pay for the goods before they're delivered) for those customers you are concerned about.

As always, the 'nine-tenths of the law is possession' rule will almost certainly apply, but be very wary indeed of entering premises to seize your goods or you could find yourself in deep trouble for trespassing. Get invited in, if only by the receptionist!

# 7. Equity

Never give away today what you can sell tomorrow!
**Jo Haigh**

Essentially, equity is the introduction of share capital into your company. Sometimes it's done directly, sometimes by way of a convertible loan – that is, the provision of the right attached to a loan that on certain conditions allows it to be converted into equity.

Providers range from wealthy investors (known as angels[1]) to huge multinationals, private equity players, venture capitalists and corporate joint venturers.

Equity is seen as risk finance – that is, finance where the reward in terms of repayment is linked to company performance. Thus, a dividend is paid if and when the company performs or where value is multiplied when the equity is sold to someone else.

Percentages paid for equity stakes can include a premium if sold to an institution or trade buyer.

Control is usually exerted in a different manner for equity facilities as opposed to debt. Usually, funders providing unsecured

[1] See Funding, section 1, p. 46

finance such as equity will have a proviso in the investment agreement that allows them to appoint a nominated director to the board to represent their interests. And due to the fact that equity has no security, the funder will be looking for a high return on their investment, which they usually achieve when the business is sold on to a third party at a later stage.

In sorting out equity, watch out for your rights in the appointment of the non-executive director who will be representing the funder. They can make or break the relationship on the deal.

I once worked with a small chain of family grocers who, following a buy-out using a well-known venture capitalist, appointed an ex-multinational superstore player to the board as their representative. This individual's knowledge did not in any way relate to the problems of a company that, whilst in the same industry, was much smaller and needed management at the micro level – which he wasn't able, or willing, to provide. It was a complete disaster; make sure it doesn't happen to you!

The subscription agreement for an equity investment will usually require you to give personal warranties about the state of the business, and to enter into covenants regarding the future running of the business, which will prevent you, for instance, from taking key decisions without the consent of the equity investor.

The major problem with equity is that smaller sums are notoriously difficult to fund – anything less than £1 million is seen as very small, while anything less than £5 million is fairly difficult to obtain. So usually, for modest sums, there is only limited access or fairly specific funders, many of whom are regional or product-focused.

What you need to do regarding equity is match the product to the need: overdraft for working capital, loans for expansion and capital expenditure and equity for growth. And for equity ensure that a clear exit is there for the provider, and that returns are potentially very high.

# 8. Executive summary

The dinosaur's eloquent lesson is that if some bigness is good, an overabundance of bigness is not necessarily better.
**Eric Johnson, President, US Chamber of Commerce**

Whether you are seeking an investment in your company, or simply looking to inform and advise your shareholders, you'll need a business plan to serve as your means of communication. And the most important part of this is the executive summary.

There's no mystery about an executive summary. It's basically a synopsis of the whole document, with enough detail to convey the key elements of the plan. But it does need to be well written, punchy and well laid out (good line spacing and lots of white space help, believe it or not).

When I'm trying to describe a good executive summary, I usually say it's like the successful blurb on the back cover of a novel – the kind that makes you buy the book as, say, you're rushing to catch a plane. If it's any good, just setting out the outline of the 'story' is enough to entice you to find out more, without giving the whole plot away!

Just bear in mind the following points:

1. Funders and investors of all kinds are inundated with opportunities, and only have a limited amount of time to investigate each one.

2. Most people initially just skim a proposal.

With these facts in mind, you need to ensure that your reader will 'buy into your plan', whether they are a potential investor or another stakeholder. Either way, your executive summary is your only chance to make a good first impression.

## Punchy and to the point

If you want to encourage a funder to invest in your business, make sure you say this, as well as how much you're looking for, within the first few paragraphs. There is nothing more annoying than wondering what the company wants from the reader and not being able to find out until page 125!

Make sure you highlight key issues either by using bold type-face or utilising pictures or graphics where relevant.

Make sure that when you mention key issues, you include a reference to where they're dealt with in the main text, with page numbers. A table of contents is important for this reason, as it allows the reader to go to the relevant page immediately.

Make it concise and to the point, leaving the reader anxious to find out more (which will naturally be found in the plan itself).

Very often, an executive summary is all someone will see in the early stages of an investment opportunity; and although it is commonplace to email such documents, sending a hard copy that can easily be written on, particularly if there are colour graphics or pictures, will have a much greater impact.

The executive summary is the first part of your plan, but it will need to be written last. Make sure that it mirrors the plan itself in form, starting with a brief history of the business and concluding with exit opportunities.

You only get one chance to make a first impression. Get it right!

# 9. Fixed and floating charges

The better work men do is always done under stress and at great personal cost.
**William Carlos Williams, American Modernist poet**

What is a charge over an asset? In effect, it is a form of security for the person who provides something, such as funding. So when you take a mortgage out on your home, you make such a charge available to your mortgage provider by allowing them to seize your home if you default on payment. A business charge is no different.

When a borrower is looking for funding, the lender is very often looking for some sort of security. The most common method is to provide a debenture.

A debenture is a recorded charge against an asset. That means that if a debt is not satisfied, then the holder or owner of the debenture can seize the asset and realise its value to do so. The signing of a debenture is a serious matter, as it is lodged at Companies House, allowing public access to what assets are secured against what, to whom and in what chronological order.

Within the registered debenture will be details of whether the charge is fixed or floating. Many funders will ask for both a fixed and floating charge (a typical 'belt and braces' approach), while others will have one or the other.

## Fixed charge

The fixed charge is the most senior charge of the two. It gives the owner of the charge a right over the asset that, if enforced, doesn't look too dissimilar to legal ownership in that in the event of a default they have absolute right to take possession and sell the asset.

A fixed charge could be over plant and equipment, but is more likely to be over buildings and land. This charge will rank in priority to a floating charge, meaning that any proceeds from the realisation of an asset held as a fixed charge will go first of all to that debenture holder.

## Floating charge

A floating charge is a little different. First of all, it is likely to apply to several assets of a business whose value may fluctuate. An example would be debtors (although whether a charge over debtors can be a fixed charge is the frequent subject of litigation[*1]), or stock – that is, items tradeable within the normal course of business.

The lender who has this charge has no immediate right over the assets, but if the charge crystallises – for instance, if the business in question goes into liquidation – they have the right to participate in the proceeds arising from that.

Confusingly, floating charges can be converted into fixed charges. This may for example occur if the business in question is being wound up. Under these circumstances if an asset has to be realised to satisfy a debt, i.e. it has to be sold, should there be a surplus of funds after the debt has been satisfied then that surplus will become subject to a floating charge! Hence the banks' frequent insistence on both a fixed and a floating charge as their security. Floating charges are paid out after fixed charges and preferential creditors have been satisfied.

Since September 2003 there have been a couple of legal changes in relation to floating charges and their validity that are worth noting.

The first is that if the floating charge was created before 15 September 2003, anything collected under that charge is payable to preferential creditors first; and if it was created after 15 September 2003, in addition a balance of the sums realised must be set aside for the unsecured creditors first. Which is interesting, as this improves the position of the trade creditor who has historically always got the crumbs, if there were any, following a liquidation!

The second is that since that same date, H M Revenue & Customs (formerly the Inland Revenue and Customs & Excise) are no longer regarded as preferential creditors (although employee outstanding pay and holiday pay arrears remain preferential). So once again unsecured creditor positions are improved, which has got to be a good thing!

[*1] See Funding, section 17, p. 46

# 10. Heads of term v. sale and purchase agreement

You can tell whether a man is clever by his answers.
You can tell whether a man is wise by his questions.
**Naguib Mahfouz, Egyptian novelist**

When you are buying or selling a business, two important documents that will occupy a considerable amount of your time and talks are the heads of term and the sale and purchase agreement. These documents are usually produced by the acquiring teams' lawyers, and form a substantial part of the agreement to carry out the transaction.

It is important, however, to realise the very considerable differences between the two.

Heads of term, sometimes referred to as a letter of intent or heads of agreement, lay out the principal terms of a possible transaction. They are fairly brief and should only contain salient issues. None of the content of this is binding, even when signed by both parties, except, usually, a confidentiality clause and an exclusivity or lock-out clause.

So it is pointless spending hours of expensive legal time arguing over the minute detail – but sadly, some lawyers seem to forget this! On umpteen occasions I have witnessed fees escalating out of all proportion to the deal, while badly advised teams hammer out details that will only be changed at a later stage.

It is perfectly true that the heads of term do form the spirit of the deal, and renegotiating on the content after due diligence (see 'Contingent fees and due diligence costs', starting on page 53) is performed is not desirable, particularly for a vendor. However, things do change – often very considerably – between agreeing the principle of a deal and actually completing!

That is not to say that you should not take advice on the content of heads of term; but don't attempt to write the **whole** agreement within them, as this will be a waste of time and money.

## Key to the deal

The sale and purchase agreement, on the other hand, is quite a different animal. This hugely important document describes in very specific detail the quantum and structure of the deal, and clarifies exactly such pertinent issues as warranties and indemnities and rights of ownership of the shares.

You are unlikely to sign this document until actual completion, but when you do, it becomes a contract enforceable in law which carries all the usual penalties for breach. Having said that, to an extent, everything and everyone has to accept some compromise in a transaction, so do try and think with a level of commerciality.

Lawyers are only doing their job when they are seeking to protect you from the remotest possibility of litigation, but at some point a degree of risk is inevitable. Make sure you are well advised of the degree of risk, then instruct accordingly.

Lawyers for the management and funders can argue for ever and a day that they want a whole raft of warranties from a venture capitalist who is also a seller, when the business is sold to the management, but the chances of getting them all is **nil** – and in the meantime, costs are escalating. Take advice and measure your own risk by enacting proper due diligence on those parts of the business you don't greatly know, and by reading and understanding the contracts **yourself**. After all, it is your money!

# 11. Joint and several liability

The best way to escape from a problem is to solve it.
**Alan Saporta, American singer**

Liability, as you'll know, simply means the state of being legally obliged to pay back another party in some way. In a business deal, avoid giving a personal guarantee[1] if at all possible. This makes sense unless you are on the other side, seeking some sort of security! At any rate, it's a wise move to try to understand the different implications of joint and several liability.

Let's look at all three possibilities:

- **Joint and several liability** basically means that you have a shared liability with a number of other people. The person with the benefit of the guarantee can choose to sue all or any one or most of the guarantors for the full amount. If any of the guarantors should be unable to make their payment in full but are asked to do so, any one of the other guarantors will be liable for the full amount. It is then up to those who have paid to get a contribution from those who have not.
- **Joint liability** provides for a legal liability against two or more people, and only allows them to be sued as a group, not individually.
- **Several liability** ensures that each person is liable for his or her share of the liability. So if four people are severally liable on an equal basis, each is liable for 25 per cent. If one can't pay their 25 per cent, the person with the benefit of the guarantee cannot pursue the others for the shortfall.

As always, be careful what you sign!

I recently noticed that my own teenage daughter's contract for student accommodation in a shared house put a joint and several liability on the tenants. If we hadn't changed this, that would have meant that should one of them not pay their rent, the others would have been liable – or, in practical terms, I would have been!

[1] See Funding, section 14, p. 72

# 12. Overdraft v. loan

The trouble with being poor is that it takes up all your time.
**Willem de Kooning**

Companies and people tend to borrow the wrong type of money. Generally, I would say it isn't their fault, but it certainly becomes their problem if things go wrong at a later date.

So the moral of this story is to match the money to the need.

## Overdrafts

The most widely provided facility available from your average high street bank is our old friend, the overdraft. How good a friend? Let's see.

An overdraft should be used to fund working capital (please note that this is not capital expenditure!). Working capital means the money needed to support your **growing** business to pay for any expansion in stock and work in progress, and to fund your growing debtor book.

With an overdraft, you should sometimes be touching your peak allowances and sometimes be in credit. Interest rates vary, depending on the security available, and the type and age of the business; but they're likely to be between 2 and 7 per cent over the base rate.

If an overdraft is being used properly, as I've noted above, it is the cheapest and most effective way of funding your business – as you only pay for the facility when you use it! But it doesn't always work out this way. If you have an overdraft of, say, £200,000 and are continually £150,000-plus overdrawn, you really should have a £150,000 loan and a £50,000 overdraft.

Why? The reasons are threefold. First, you will probably be able to negotiate a better rate for a loan, so it's cheaper, provided you use it properly. Secondly, the banks feel more secure with a loan. For one thing, they have a payment plan in place, and for another, they probably have better-quality security against, say, a specific asset.

And thirdly, and usually very importantly, an overdraft facility will almost always have a linked right to instant recall, as well as the right to appoint a receiver or administrator to handle it. Neither of which are pleasant experiences and both of which are outside your personal control!

So it's a little disheartening that banks have an inclination to push you towards an overdraft – particularly during the early stages of setting up your business or if you're in a new start-up company – on the basis that it's much quicker to arrange than a loan and that they can simply recall it if it all goes pear-shaped.

## Loans

Loans are available from a multitude of sources, with many local as well as national and regional providers, which aren't necessarily related to the core banking community. They have a variety of structures, in terms of security, repayment and interest patterns, so it's a must to shop around for the one that suits.

The periods available for paying back the loan are also variable to some extent, depending on the type of security attached to them. For instance, building loans can attract terms of up to 25 years, whereas a car loan is likely to have a maximum term of, say, five years and everything else is in between. The key is to match the term to the life of the asset wherever possible.

Also check penalty clauses for early redemption and novation rights (the right to transfer the debt to a third party). In other words, be aware of what happens to the loan/facility if there is a change of ownership of the asset, which will happen, for instance, if you sell your company.

Rates for loans tend to vary between 1 and 5 per cent over base, but are subject to the usual caveats of age and type of business, and so on.

# 13. Performance bonds

A fool and his money are soon parted.
**Thomas Tusser, *Five Hundred Points of Good Husbandry***

A performance bond's main purpose is to ensure that a contract undertaken will be completed satisfactorily. It guarantees that the contractual obligations will be met. When you're trying to secure a contract, providing a performance bond can offer a great advantage if your competitor is unwilling or unable to provide one. And if you're provided with one, it offers a real sense of security.

These bonds can be given by the contractor, although clearly they need to be underwritten by a sound financial source in this case; or alternatively, they can be provided by a specialist financier.

All sorts of rights can be attached to bonds, including step-in rights. These effectively give the holder the right to take over the contract if there is a default.

Clearly, the wording of these documents and the financial security behind them are both massively important.

Performance bonds are mostly used in the construction industry, but that doesn't in any way preclude their use in other businesses.

Where a performance bond can come into its own for a provider is that they do not necessarily reduce available bank facilities, although this won't always be so. But the alternative is to allocate specific funds to an escrow account (an account that only the advisers of both parties can access), so a bond is obviously more attractive, at least on the face of it.

If you're contemplating offering such a bond, I'd ask your advisers for help and advice.

# 14. Personal guarantees

> The safe way to double your money is to fold it over
> once and put it in your pocket.
> **Frank 'Kin' Hubbard, American cartoonist**

It is not unusual for a funder to ask a director or a group of directors to personally guarantee the repayment of a facility – the
amount of money you have available, such as an overdraft – if the
company is unable to do so. But the extent of the guarantee and
the way it is given need consideration.

Once a funder has a guarantee, a degree of resistance to
releasing it often seems to develop. Even when the requirement no
longer exists, experience shows that banks rarely, if ever, remind
you of the guarantee's existence.

## Setting limits

Therefore if you must provide a guarantee, one tip is to limit it
time-wise. You could, for instance, make it voidable at each
facility renewal date, leaving you at least the opportunity to rene-
gotiate the terms of any further renewals, although banks will be
very reluctant to agree this unconditionally.

Certainly you should limit the amount of the guarantee wherever possible. An unlimited guarantee effectively means you will
have to cover all future losses that the funder may find unrecoverable from another source.

Beware of joint and several guarantees[1] between a group of
guarantors. That 'joint and several' basically means you may
end up picking up any shortfalls if your colleagues are unable
to liquidate their assets at sufficient speed – or simply don't
have any.

Finally, be aware of some very pertinent case law in relation to

[1] See Funding, section 1, p. 67

the validity of a personal guarantee. RBS v Etridge stated that for a guarantee to be binding, your domestic partner must have taken separate and independent legal advice and have a clear understanding of the implications of the guarantee.

In short, very often for a new or newish business with a limited trading history, a personal guarantee is essential to secure the funding. But that doesn't mean you shouldn't negotiate on the structure and extent of it!

# 15. Small Firm Loans Guarantee Scheme (SFLGS)

I'd like to live as a poor man with lots of money.
**Pablo Picasso**

Small businesses have been able to access finance secured by the UK government since 1981, when the Department of Trade and Industry introduced the Small Firm Loans Guarantee Scheme (SFLGS). This is a godsend for smaller companies, as they tend to lack available collateral to secure funding for their further development, and this is a way of drawing down the necessary finance.

This is important for the country as a whole, not just the companies in question. Because the UK is still largely a nation built on relatively modest businesses, they play a vital part in national prosperity.

As with any government initiative there are lots of caveats, including turnover and industry limitations as well as guarantee percentages. These, along with amounts that can be drawn down, are revisited periodically by the government.

Currently the guarantee percentage is 70 or 85 per cent – the latter only being available for companies with two plus years of trading. Rates are usually base rate plus 1.5 per cent for a variable rate or 0.5 per cent for a fixed rate.

Although in theory few business sectors are specifically excluded, start-up companies and small businesses have the most difficulty securing the funding, with retail and high-tech businesses rarely qualifying.

## How to access SFLGS

Most high street banks provide access to the SFLGS along with various regional and specific lenders, such as:

| | |
|---|---|
| Bank of Ireland (Northern Ireland only) | Northern Enterprise |
| Bank of Scotland | Northern Investors Company Limited |
| Barclays Bank | oneLondon Limited |
| Clydesdale Bank | Royal Bank of Scotland |
| Co-operative Bank | State Securities PLC |
| Doncaster Business Advice Centre | Triodos Bank |
| Emerging Business Trust Limited | UK Steel Enterprise |
| First Trust Bank/Allied Irish Bank | Ulster Bank Limited |
| HSBC Bank | Venture Finance PLC |
| Lloyds TSB Group PLC | Yorkshire Bank |
| National Westminster Bank | Yorkshire Enterprise Limited |
| Northern Bank Limited | |

Loans are available from periods of between two and ten years on sums for £5,000 to £100,000 (up to £250,000 if your business has been trading for more than two years). Note that to be eligible for an SFLG you must be a UK company with an annual turnover of no more than £3 million (£5 million if you are a manufacturer).

You will need to demonstrate a viable business case which the funder wants to support, and which only your lack of security prevents you from getting off the ground. (Security, by the way, includes your own **personal** security.)

Inside tip – if your domestic partner is not prepared to sign over your house as security, this may not be classed as an available asset.

# 16. Specialised lending/ intensive care banking

> When a feller says it ain't the money but the principle
> of the thing, it's the money.
> **Abe Martin, cartoon character of Kin Hubbard**

You might think intensive care is what you can expect to get after major, life-threatening surgery. Not always. Whatever a particular bank may call it (and that might be 'specialised lending'), most high street lenders also have an intensive care department.

The role of this banking department or managerial group is to look after a business that's on the brink, for whatever reason. They could aim to minimise banking exposure in terms of exiting from the lend as soon as possible or they could try to manage the lend through to a more secure position.

There has always been the valid argument that if you owe the bank £10 million, they have a problem; whereas if you owe the bank £1 million, you have a problem! (The amounts, of course, are moveable, dependent on risk.)

If your bank begins to worry about the security of the amount they've lent you, very often they will commission a third party, usually a firm of accountants, to carry out a so-called impartial investigation into your performance.

## End in sight?

Nine times out of ten, this is the kiss of death for your company. If the report tells the bank to get out, then generally if they can, they will – they are in business, after all. But sometimes it may not be possible to exit in as fine a state as is desirable. So the next option may be to move the account to a specialist team.

Several things can happen if this occurs.

The bank may, for instance, take a slug of your equity – in other words, ownership of a part of your company. They will almost certainly start monitoring your account, which may well include the appointment of a director to your board; and for this they will charge a monitoring fee, which is automatically deducted from your account.

On top of this, all sorts of covenants will be introduced, which may include restrictions on directors' benefits and even trading conditions.

The provision of timely information and a good communication programme will help you enormously with managing what can be a very upsetting experience. So if this happens to you, start as you mean to go on. You **must** build a good relationship very quickly with these people if you want to retain any degree of hope about your company.

One recent client had been told that when they moved his account to specialised lending it was because these managers had the specialist sector experience the branch didn't have. Needless to say, this was not quite true!

# 17. The Brumark case

Laws are like sausages, it is better not to see them being made.
**Otto von Bismarck**

Do you have a bank account or other funding facility, and is this secured by a debenture (a charge) on your assets – in particular, your debtor book? If your answer is yes, read on.

The effect of the Brumark case, a Privy Council ruling, is very significant for corporate borrowers.

Banks generally dislike lending without security, and a common lending mechanism is to take security against specific assets, which very often is your debtor book. What that means is that when a default occurs, the charge that the bank has taken as security is realised and used to pay the debt to the bank.

If such debts can be the subject of a fixed charge, they are more valuable as security than if they can only rank as a floating charge (see page 63). This is because money realised through a floating charge asset can only be used after preferential creditors (the ones with a right to be paid first, should the company go into liquidation) are paid. For some years there have been legal cases to try to work out whether a charge over book debts – that is, money owed for services or products already delivered – can be a fixed charge or can only now be a floating charge.

## What the decision means

The Brumark decision said that the charge could become fixed only if the bank were in control of the sales ledger, including its collection and the proceeds of book debts. So in most cases, charges over book debts will only be floating charges.

The banks have three ways of dealing with this dilemma:

1. They don't give the facility in the first place (not a good business development technique).

2. They take extra security either on other assets within the business or as personal security from the director.

OR

3. They persuade the business to either factor or invoice discount its debts (this way there is no charge given, as the bank actually takes ownership of the ledger).

To clarify the terminology here, factoring means selling your sales invoices to a third party (the factor), who pays you a percentage of the value before the due date; the factor then collects the rest of the debt and pays you the balance less their costs. The process is similar to invoice discounting in that a prepayment is made to the company by the specialist lender, but the company who sold the product collects the debt, and payment is made to that company by the customer; the company then makes a payment retrospectively for the cost of borrowing.

However, factoring and invoice discounting aren't applicable for all businesses, so this option may be a nonstarter. At this point, you can probably see where this is all heading.

Banks may have no option but to take only a floating charge, which will not necessarily give them priority over other preferential creditors. Privy Council rulings are not yet law and won't be until someone takes a test case to the House of Lords (watch this space) – but undoubtedly banks are taking this on board, and the wording in debentures is being carefully examined.

Banks are also trying, wherever possible, to manage this greater perceived risk, and interest rate hikes – along with personal guarantees – are more likely than ever before.

All this calls for a creative approach to funding solutions to maximise available debt and minimise director risks.

# 18. Venture capital specifics re: deal, non-executive directors

Do not ask your venture capitalist to explain what he's doing or why.
**A. J. Carroll, *Bluff Your Way in Tax***

Investment is a many-splendoured thing. But any company that takes third-party institutional investment into their business is, by and large, entering into a type of marital arrangement from which obtaining a divorce is both very painful and frightfully expensive. So choose your bride with care!

In this case, the 'brides' are merchant banks, venture capitalists and private equity players eager for a stake in your company's shareholding, in exchange for venture capital. This is, in essence, funding for companies that carry a fair amount of investment risk but promise above-average rewards later.

Every venture capital deal is different, but what most have in common is a desire to exit the investment at a given point – rarely after more than five years – and to do so at a very large premium! Along the route to exit, the venture capitalists in question will also be looking to take a substantial return on what they see as risk capital.

## Specifics of the case

The first specific, therefore, is not to expect this money to come cheaply, as return expectations are very high (mostly due to the high number of failures!).

Note, however, that the cost of such transactions is only part of the issue, and indeed should not be used in itself as a deciding factor in choosing one particular investor or another. As these deals are so often collaborative and relationship-based, the philosophy and mindset of the venture capitalist is very important.

The second specific is that it's a rare investor indeed who does not appoint a nominee non-executive director to represent their interests on your board. These individuals (who incidentally are usually funded by your company, not the venture capitalist), can make or break deals, particularly when things get difficult – and they often do! So you need to carefully consider who they are, what they do and how much you are expected to pay them.

Nine times out of ten you will be given a choice of personnel (check your investment agreement criteria regarding this issue), and clearly it is in everyone's interest to make the relationship work. But while in the legal sense, these people have the same duty of care to the company as you do, they are representing the venture capitalists, and this is inevitably a difficult line to tread.

How much should you pay for this person's services, usually for about 12 to 15 days a year? Again, this does depend on deal size and type to some extent, but don't expect any change out of at least £25,000 per year for a medium-sized business.

Experience shows that you won't see your investment manager for dust when things are going well – but when and if you hit a rocky patch, the picture changes dramatically! And as many of these investment managers have a financial background, expect to experience the interesting phenomenon of an accountant running your business.

That said, the third specific regarding an investment from a venture capitalist is first of all to negotiate hard on the covenants they place on you as part of the investment – then manage them like mad.

A good tip to know in this context is that venture capitalists, like banks in general, don't like unpleasant surprises. So as poor as the potential future may seem, you are well advised to communicate this fact to your investor well in advance rather than just wait until it happens. They will be much more likely to support you then, if and when things go wrong.

The venture capitalist isn't readily going to allow you to change your business focus. So a fourth specific is to make sure you are entirely happy with any restrictions placed on what the company can and can't do that may be contained in the objects clause*1 of your Memorandum and Articles of Association, as amending these will inevitably need their permission!

Finally: whatever they say, everything in a transaction is negotiable. And that means everything!

If they want the deal, there are always compromises to be made. Draw up a must have and a wish list. The latter contains items you may be willing to compromise on, the first list those that you're not.

*1 See Structure, section 11, p. 26

An investment backed by a venture capitalist can be a wonderful opportunity, because it can get a deal off the ground that wouldn't be airborne otherwise. But go into it with your eyes wide open and negotiate hard at the start, as later on you may not be in such a favourable position.

# Compliance: knowing what's mandatory

The incestuous relationship between government and big business thrives in the dark.
**Jack Anderson, journalist and Mormon missionary**

If you knew everything there was to know about starting a business, you might choose to back off from the idea altogether. So a soupçon of ignorance can be relative bliss. But on the other hand, taking on too many ostrich tendencies is clearly not desirable – particularly when it comes to compliance with laws and regulations.

UK business legislation is a constantly changing arena, and statutes, case law and European regulations and directives impinge on our lives on a daily basis.

Just to add another knot to this tangled situation, case law – the mechanism largely used to interpret statutes – is subject to an appeal process which can reverse and re-reverse previous decisions. Laws can end up appearing to be made retrospectively. So it's entirely feasible that you could breach these laws by mistake!

But ignorance of the law is never an excuse. So what can you do to improve your knowledge?

# Getting informed

There are lots and lots of seminars available from lawyers and accountants from Business Link (see www.businesslink.gov.uk, or call 0845 600 9 006, to find your local link), and specialists such as health and safety providers, so take advantage of these. There is also support available from trade organisations – often offered 'free' as part of your membership fee.

Some firms will provide a compliance health check on these issues. There may be a cost attached to this, but for peace of mind and to avoid possible litigation implications, it is well worth considering.

As more and more lawyers act on a 'no win, no fee' basis, many plaintiffs feel they have little to lose in bringing an action. And even if their lawyer will not act pro bono (without charging a fee), there may be legal aid or union support for an action.

However, try to avoid litigation wherever possible. It is harrowing and expensive for most people – even if you win the case!

# Who holds the reins?

Many compliance issues fall in the remit of the company secretary. Although in a private company (as opposed to a PLC) such a person needs no qualifications, they still have lots of potential liabilities. I recommend that you think very carefully about who holds this role, and possibly even consider asking your professional advisers – that is, your accountants or solicitors – to fill the position.

Largely, however, the buck stops with the board, and it is you who will be disqualified or worse if you are non-compliant. So you must seek help and ensure that you keep up to date in all the relevant areas. You can delegate, but you must not abdicate.

As with most things, many compliance matters seem cumbersome and tiresome and the truth is they will only come back to haunt you when something goes wrong. But the law of averages says that when it does go wrong, it is most likely to go spectacularly wrong; and a non-compliance could be a potential disaster for you and your business.

The moral? Be informed – and compliant!

# 1. Business, the internet and the law

I do not fear computers. I fear the lack of them.
**Isaac Asimov, science fiction writer whose works include**
***I, Robot***

Internet trading is here to stay – and stay big time. The last few years have seen a supernova-style explosion in this area, and the law has not quite managed to keep up to speed with all the developments. This isn't helped by the global scope of the internet, which makes it difficult to say, at the very least, which country's law applies to any dispute.

And as we've seen, the law doesn't stand still either. Recent disability discrimination laws, for instance, make it an offence for you not to make reasonable adjustments to your website to ensure that the disabled have equal access.

## Key issues online

Protecting your trademark is something you will definitely want to consider. Register all your brands as domain names to avoid someone else taking it – if you're not too late already. Don't forget to include disclaimers and copyright statements on websites, or you will be liable for people acting on your advice (see 'Intellectual property', starting on page 21).

*1 See Compliance, section 7, p. 92

With e-commerce trading and possibly other areas you will be governed by the Data Protection Act,[*1] and you should consider using tick boxes to allow users to choose whether they want to be involved in mailings from you or others in the future.

If you use hyperlinks on your site, check out the legality of the link to avoid liability issues.

If you are making sales on the web you will also be covered by the Distance Selling Regulations (for consumers only), and advice on pricing, order confirmation and cooling-off periods are very strict. (Cooling off is the period of time after contracts have been exchanged, during which, depending on type of contract, it can be cancelled. The period is usually five working days.) The Department of Trade and Industry (DTI) has a distance selling guide which is certainly worth a look.

Finally, the Electronic Commerce Regulation applies to any business that operates online using emails. Again, the DTI has a guide. This covers matters such as the requirement to clearly state the name of your company, VAT number, company registration number and other essential details on your website. Non-compliance is taken very seriously, so take specialist advice.

# 2. Contracts of employment

The harder you work, the luckier you get.
**McAlexander, writer**

After two calendar months of employment, everyone has a legal entitlement to a contract of employment. If they do not get a written one from their employer, they will certainly be presumed to have an implied one.

The number of hours an employee works is irrelevant. Whether it's one hour or 60 hours, a written statement is required.

[*1] See Compliance, section 3, p. 87

Along with the names of the relevant parties involved, there are a number of other basics that need to appear in this document. It needs to state the start date of the employment, how the person will be paid, and details of holiday, sick leave and pension arrangements. A brief job description should be included. The place of work should also be specified, but be careful: if this is made specific, a relocation of any distance could create a redundancy or constructive dismissal claim. Notice periods and disciplinary rules also need reference, bearing in mind the statutory disciplinary requirements, which must not be breached.

Where you have individuals who need to work outside the UK for more than a month, this also needs to be stated explicitly along with any provision for payment to be made in anything other then sterling.

Clear reference needs to be made about terms and conditions relating to an employee's return to the UK if they work overseas periodically.

## Avoiding dismissal pitfalls

Amendments to contracts need careful negotiation to avoid constructive dismissal claims, which would result in successful unfair dismissal claims. Any amendment to job terms done without consultation, or excessive demotion – such as making an office manager an office junior – could both be construed as constructive dismissal.

The best advice is to take advice.

Unfair dismissal claims are index linked, and can exceed £50,000. So failing to manage your people and processes effectively could amount to an expensive mistake.

Here's an inside tip. Most people have a clause that gross misconduct allows you to dismiss the employee. But however gross the misconduct, you must follow procedure. That means suspension followed by investigation, followed by review and appeal. If you don't, your claim that you dismissed them properly because of the act outlined in the contract may fail!

This happened to a friend. He summarily dismissed his foreman for drinking alcohol while using dangerous machinery – but lost the case, as he had not suspended, investigated, and so on.

So be careful and remember to follow the procedures.

# 3. Data protection

Few things can help an individual more than to place responsibility on him, and to let him know that you trust him.

**Booker T. Washington, *Up from Slavery***

Although the Data Protection Act of 1998 has had its share of critics (not least of which is the Court of Appeal), it is there to protect us from what is seemingly becoming a surveillance society.

It provides the legal basis for protecting the private, personal data of individuals and businesses in the UK. Under it, data disclosed by one party to another can only be used for the purpose it was disclosed for; and without the consent of the owner of the data, it can't be disclosed to other parties. The Data Protection Registrar oversees the implementation of the Act.

Unfortunately, it isn't possible to provide a list of dos and don'ts in relation to the Act. So companies will need to apply commonsense principles when dealing with private and personal information.

You may be surprised to know that it is the official receiver who is the data controller for the Act in relation to the potential disqualification of a director. As such, the official receiver can access and verify information concerning individuals, although they cannot disclose the information to third parties outside the

Insolvency Service unless there is legal provision. (The Insolvency Service, an executive agency of the DTI, deals with corporate and individual insolvency, and investigates fraud and misconduct, in England, Wales and some parts of Scotland.)

As information held on you could, of course, be very detrimental, you are allowed to know which information is being accessed unless the official receiver believes that may prejudice his case. It is certainly worth checking that what is held is accurate, and you can do this by contacting the data protection liaison officers at the official receiver's office.

There is a data protection helpline, 01625 545745, which is geared to company needs, and also a very good website, www.informationcommissioner.gov.uk, for businesses that need help interpreting the Act.

## Good practice under the Act

The essence of the Act is to allow individuals to access their personal information. Anyone who processes data must register with the Data Protection Register (this is virtually every type of business, so it's best to check).

Some general good practice principles would be to:

1. Get the permission of the individual concerned before processing data containing information on them

2. Be accurate in terms of content and try to keep information to the minimum.

Anyone seeking to review their information must be given sight of the data within 40 days. Failure to provide this, subject to certain conditions, is in itself a criminal offence.

# 4. Declaration of interests

Connected persons – most relatives of a taxpayer, plus
maids, but excluding lovers and mistresses.
**From the Chartered Institute of Taxation website**

If you make sure that you act properly at meetings in relation to any issue in which you may have a potential interest, it can only be a good thing. Not only will your general corporate governance be improved, but it could help prevent you from breaking the law (even if you had no intention to do so!).

The bottom line is that you should declare your interests at all meetings where matters are being discussed that affect them. The words 'your interests' also cover associated persons, including your domestic partner, children, step-children and, to be safe indeed, any relative. And it includes any organisation in which you hold a 20 per cent or more interest.

Clearly, you only need to declare an interest you know about. You have no obligation to investigate the business interests of your friends and relatives.

Good practice says you should declare and give details of your interest in the matter as soon as it becomes apparent to you – ideally at the start of the meeting, provided you are aware of it. And you should make such a declaration even if you maintain a register of interests.

Once your interest has been noted, you should not participate in either the discussion or vote unless the Articles of Association allow you to do so. Indeed, some schools of thought would recommend that you withdraw from the meeting for the duration of the discussion to allow for free, unbiased debate.

This may all seem rather formal and cumbersome, but you must remember that as a director it is essential that you are always seen to be acting in the best interests of **the company** rather than gaining as a director. At a later stage you may need to prove this, and there is nothing like written minutes to give you a good start.

Even if you are a sole director or shareholder, you should note that you have declared your interest to yourself! This may seem rather strange; but it has been the subject of a case in the courts, where the declaration of interest was defined as providing time for reflection.

# 5. Directors' loans

> Annual income twenty pounds, annual expenditure
> nineteen pounds and six, result happiness. Annual
> income twenty pounds, annual expenditure twenty
> pounds and six, result misery.
> **Charles Dickens, *David Copperfield***

Although it is entirely acceptable for a director to lend money to the company he works for, it is not possible (except for limited amounts up to £5,000 and for business-related activities) to borrow money from your company where you hold a directorship.

This restriction applies not just to the provision of the loan itself, but also the guaranteeing or the provision of an indemnity or security against a loan. The restriction also applies to transactions with directors of certain other group companies, and includes shadow directors.[1]

But what are the penalties for breaking this law?

If the loan exceeds 10 per cent of the business's net assets, your auditors are obliged to file a report with the Office of the Director of Corporate Enforcement (ODCE). If the ODCE forms an opinion that an indictable offence has been committed, and this is proven, you will be automatically disqualified as a director.

[1] See Structure, section 17, p. 37

You should also note that the auditors themselves do not have a choice in this matter: failure to report is in itself an indictable offence!

Hundreds of cases to do with directors' loans are reported each year. A guide is available from the ODCE on www.odce.ie, and this is well worth reading – not least to note that if you breach the guidelines, you will also incur fines and up to five years in prison!

There are also tax implications both for the director and the company. First, the director will have to pay income tax on the interest-free loan he has received; and secondly, the company will incur a separate tax charge.

So don't do it!

# 6. Directors' report

Success on any major scale requires you to accept responsibility ... [In] the final analysis, the one quality that all successful people have ... is the ability to take on responsibility.
**Michael Korda, influential book publisher**

If you are a company director, you are responsible for producing an annual report for inclusion with your accounts. This provides a chronicle of the company's development during that financial year.

The annual report is the report of all the board, so you should ensure you are happy with its content. Any negligent (and of course fraudulent) statements will be regarded as a statement of all the directors.

In smaller businesses, the company auditors often write the directors' report, but it will still be regarded as your work. Ideally you should review this as a board, and approve it for inclusion in the accounts.

Any director can sign the report. The accounts are usually signed by the company secretary on behalf of the board of directors.

Some tips on what to include in the information relate to director share transfers. If, for instance, senior members of the board have either bought or sold a glut of shares, they may know something you don't (or it could mean nothing at all!).

You also need to ascertain if a company is a close company – that is, one owned and run by five or fewer people. With this number of people, the shareholders and directors are likely to be one and the same, implying a possible conflict of interest between shareholders' requirements and a director's legal duties. Many private limited companies fall into this category. Usually it means very little but it is worth having at the back of your mind when analysing a business.

# 7. Disability: discrimination

If we do not maintain justice, justice will not maintain us.
**Francis Bacon**

From October 2004, some major changes to the Disability Discrimination Act came into place. Not only is it now a specific requirement that anyone who provides a service must **actively** take steps to make their services accessible to everyone, but employers have to be very careful indeed to avoid disability discrimination. And this applies to all employers, regardless of how many staff they have.

The essence of the legislation is to consider whether the employer has made reasonable adjustments to prevent the discrimination from occurring. The organisation's size, although not irrelevant, will not be a legitimate reason in itself for failing to take action; neither is cost in itself.

All sorts of organisations who were originally excluded from the legislation are now included. The police and fire brigade are among them, although the armed forces are still excluded.

Under the new procedures, unlawful discrimination is defined as:

- Treating a disabled person less favourably for a reason related to their disability
- Failing to make reasonable adjustments to prevent the disability from compromising the job holder
- Victimising a person who has either brought or supported a person who had made a claim of disability discrimination.

## Definitions and adjustments

To prevent discrimination, you first need to define what a disability is. In addition to physical conditions such as, say, hearing impairment or multiple sclerosis, depression and dyslexia are both regarded as disabilities. So do think very carefully about the less obvious conditions. If someone brings a claim, there is no limit on compensation, and no qualifying employment periods are needed.

The second key consideration relates to the type of adjustment you may reasonably be expected to make. These include not only physical adjustments, say to work premises, but also task reallocation, job swaps, managing working hours or providing support from readers or interpreters.

> In one case, a litigant who was partially sighted won his case against a company who turned him down for a video editor's job on account of his disability. They had not even looked to see whether any adjustments could be made.

The only cases where you can successfully argue that it is legitimate to treat a disabled person differently is when the health and safety of the person or other persons would be endangered, or if the disabled person cannot give consent because of their disability.

You need to think about your recruitment and selection process, too. For instance:

- How do you draw up your job descriptions?
- Where do you interview and how?
- Where do you place your advertisements?

And once someone with a disability has taken up a position, take care over how you record any absence due to health reasons. You'll need to differentiate between disability-related absence and ordinary sick leave because while disabled people generally don't take any more sick leave than any other employee, they may need to take extra days off for disability-related reasons. You will need to make adjustments to accommodate these absences, for instance in the provision of long-term absences, sick pay entitlements and the like.

By the way, it would be regarded as very bad practice indeed to include the question 'Do you have a disability?' on an application form. It is much better to state that should the applicant require any adjustments, provisions will be made to allow a discussion to take place.

# 8. Filing accounts

Talk of nothing but business, and dispatch that business quickly.
**Aldus Manutius**

Filing accounts is, to a huge degree, about timing. You'll need to pay scrupulous attention to deadlines when you file.

The board of directors and the company secretary have legal responsibilities for the filing of accounts along with the various other annual returns. These are personal liabilities – meaning the individuals can be **personally** prosecuted – are for late filing as well as failure to file.

Filing periods are ten months from your year's end for private companies, and seven months for public companies. With first-time filing by a new company for a 12-month period, you have 22 months from incorporation for private companies, and 19 months for public companies.

The penalties for non-compliance can be very heavy and are weighted according to the time delay.

For private companies who file more than 12 months late, the penalty is £1,000 for the company. Individual directors can, however, be personally fined up to £5,000 each and a criminal prosecution can be sought, which if successful will leave the director with a criminal record and could result in a disqualification. That means you won't be able to be a director of any company for a minimum of two years to a maximum of 15 years.

You can, of course, alter your designated year's end as often as you like by shortening the period, but there are restrictions on extending the time.

## Limits and extensions

An accounting period may not extend beyond 18 months, and you can't extend more than once in five years unless:

a) The company is under an administration order (where a director or creditor puts the business under the control of a third party, so it can still trade while the debt payment is being arranged)

b) The Secretary of State has authorised it

OR

c) You are aligning your accounts date to a subsidiary or parent company established in the European Union.

For peace of mind, a smaller company should consider delegating the filing of reports to their auditors. However, don't forget – ultimately, the responsibility is still yours!

# 9. Freedom of information

That which today calls itself science gives us more and more information, an indigestible glut of information, and less and less understanding.
**Edward Abbey, American author noted for his criticism of public land policies**

The UK's Freedom of Information Act 2005 came fully into force in January 2005. Since then, all public bodies have been bound to provide and publish information, subject to certain exceptions.

Certain kinds of information, such as minutes or reports, may be proactively published together by the organisation and made available on request. And they will have to adhere to such a request if the cost of responding is less than £600.

The right of access to the information is subject to the rules under the Data Protection Act,[1] meaning generally that only the person concerned can have access to information about themselves, and not third parties, for personal data.

Requests for information must be dealt with in 20 days and provide for access to actual records, rather than mere information. The idea is to remove any subjective interpretation of the facts.

If you wish to access information and you're dissatisfied with how you are being treated during the process, you can communicate this directly to the Information Commissioner, who is responsible for enforcing the Act; and beyond that, to a tribunal or to the court on legal points.

[1] See Compliance, section 3, p. 87

# 10. Harassment and the employment equality regulations

... a new nation, conceived in Liberty, and dedicated to the proposition that all men are created equal.
**Abraham Lincoln, *The Gettysburg Address***

From December 2003, when the Employment Equality (Sexual Orientation) Regulations came into force, it became an offence to treat someone differently because of their religion, religious beliefs or sexual orientation.

Although this doesn't cover a person's political beliefs, it does include nonbelievers and specifically mentions Jedi Knights (since the 2001 census, a very popular religion!). You should be aware there is no requirement for the individual to have to prove his religion or otherwise.

In relation to sexual orientation, this includes the gay community, transvestites and transsexuals, but excludes any manifestation of that orientation such as sadism.

This area is a 'no-tolerance zone', meaning the tribunal and courts will not accept **any level** of discrimination. Don't forget that employers are vicariously liable for all their employees, so if one of your staff breaks these regulations – **you and your company will be liable.**

## The forms of discrimination

The forms of discrimination in this area are fourfold.

First there is direct discrimination. This basically means that if you treat someone in a less favourable manner because they have a religious belief or sexual orientation you disagree with – whether you just think you know or are absolutely sure – you are discriminating against them.

A recent case saw a successful claimant prove discrimination when the firm would not allow for his prayer periods within their set pattern of breaks during the day.

Secondly, there is indirect discrimination. If your business practices, such as dress codes, work breaks, social events and so on are seen to put someone of a particular religion or sexual orientation at a disadvantage, once again you are discriminating.

Thirdly – and perhaps of most concern – is harassment. This area involves you or your staff engaging in any unwanted conduct which has the purpose or effect of violating the dignity of another person. This can include office banter that isn't actually aimed at the offended person!

Recently, a devout Christian objected violently to the continued usage of 'Oh Jesus Christ' as an expletive, and won his case.

Finally, there is victimisation and post-employment discrimination. Examples would include giving inappropriate references to an ex-employee, or disciplining different people in an inconsistent manner.

Be very careful indeed in this area. Consider diversity training to ensure that you and your staff are aware of all the issues involved.

# 11. Health and safety

The law isn't justice. It's a very imperfect mechanism.
If you press exactly the right buttons and are also
lucky, justice may show up in the answer. A mechanism
is all the law was ever intended to be.
**Raymond Chandler, *The Long Goodbye***

It would be possible to write a whole book, or indeed several books, on a director's responsibility for health and safety. This summary tries to capture the salient points.

First of all, health and safety offences can be criminal offences. Criminal offences can involve very serious penalties, including loss of liberty and being barred from holding a director's role because of disqualification.

It is true that everyone in an organisation has a personal responsibility for health and safety. But directors have a special role in ensuring that health and safety guidelines are set and adhered to. In fact, the Health and Safety Executive (HSE) goes as far as recommending that each company appoints a board director who will have special responsibilities for health and safety.

The HSE also make it quite clear that they expect companies and individual directors to be very well versed in health and safety matters and to ensure that this is no mere bluff when ensuring compliance. In other words, a board's actions and decisions should visibly demonstrate the company's backing of health and safety principles.

The health and safety of your employees is clearly vital, and you may find, depending on how you run the company, that you are responsible for staff both on and off your premises. For instance, if some of your staff work at home, you'll need to carry out a risk assessment of their premises. If you haven't, and they trip over a computer lead trailing across their bedroom floor while working on your spreadsheets, for instance, it will be you and your company who will be liable.

The management of health and safety is about procedures, implementation and monitoring, and ultimately it is the directors' responsibility to ensure that procedures are adhered to – and if they aren't, that actions are taken.

## Taking it seriously

Although more junior staff may have responsibilities for health and safety, unless they are properly trained, supported and monitored, the liability for injuries will simply pass to the board and even particular directors. Quite simply, you will never be too junior to be liable if you are a member of a board that is in dereliction of its duties.

Health and safety does not just cover those industries involving heavy equipment, dangerous chemicals and the like. It can just as easily be an important issue for a small service office.

There is a substantial amount of free and cost-effective advice from any number of organisations. And the more advice you take, the better able you'll be to prove you were properly informed. For starters, try Business Hotline Publications (www.bizhot.co.uk), DTI – business best practice (www.ukonlineforbusiness.gov.uk), the Small Business Advice Service 2005 (www.smallbusinessadvice.org.uk) and Business Link (www.businesslink.gov.uk).

The Heath and Safety at Work Act has one very important statement for you: 'That you, as well as the body corporate, will be liable for the act or omission that results in a breach of the legislation.' That means that not only your company, but you personally, can be prosecuted.

# 12. Human Rights Act

I am only one; but still I am one. I cannot do everything, but still I can do something; I will not refuse to do something I can do.
**Helen Keller, deaf and blind author, activist and lecturer**

The UK was one of the last European countries to bring in its own Human Rights Act, which came into force in October 2000. Before this, the only recourse for anyone in the UK who believed their human rights had been infringed was the Court of Human Rights in Strasbourg!

So since October 2000, it has been possible to bring an action directly to a UK court. And the Act has even wider ramifications: it is generally seen as an influencing Act, which means that its interpretation by case law will generate change in customs and practice, and expand the Act's own scope.

From the perspective of employment law, the Act has some very relevant articles that need consideration.

# Key articles of the Act

Article 3 relates to the prohibition of torture or degrading treatment. I imagine, and certainly hope, that torture is rare in business in the UK, but 'degrading treatment' could be seen to relate to such matters as the right to search someone. So if this is an area that affects your business because of any products or services you produce, the question that would be asked is whether you, as employer, behaved reasonably under the circumstances of such a search.

Article 4 relates to slavery, and specifically regarding employment issues, to forced labour. The area you need to look at here is ensuring that any trial employment, for instance, is properly recompensed.

Article 5 concerns the right of liberty and security of a person. Those businesses that detain people on their own volition, for instance care homes, will need to ensure they have considered the implications of the article in relation to their practices.

Article 6 relates to the right to a fair trial. If someone is sacked with less than a year's service and without going through proper disciplinary procedures, it could possibly be said that they haven't had access to the same assistance in terms of disciplinary support as someone with 12 months' employment. So although they might not have an unfair dismissal claim, that won't exclude a human rights claim!

Article 8 relates to privacy. Issues likely to fall within this area could include monitoring of emails and phone calls, although the law does allow for this in certain circumstances. The key is to ensure that such monitoring will only take place with the knowledge and/or agreement of those involved. Anything covert may be regarded as entrapment and be inadmissible as evidence.

Article 10 is about your freedom of expression. There have already been a number of successful cases relating to dress codes and the like, so be very careful in terms of what is mandatory. The term 'business attire' may well be acceptable, but insisting on collar and tie for the men in your firm may not be!

Finally, Article 14 relates to the general prohibition of discrimination on the grounds of sex, race and disability, age and sexual orientation. Although these issues are now covered in the Employment Equality (Sexual Orientation) Regulations (see 'Harassment and the employment equality regulations', starting on page 97), be aware that this article stands in addition to such rights, and could potentially result in a double action in the case of a breach.

There has been a general escalation of cases since the Act, so review your procedures in these areas. Non-compliance is an expensive mistake.

# 13. Illegal dividends

Lawyers and painters can soon turn white to black.
**Danish proverb**

Paying remuneration to directors via a dividend (a share of the profits available to a shareholder who is also a director) has long been used as a tax-effective tool. However, you will be in breach of the Companies Act if you pay a dividend without sufficient profit reserves. (Reserves are not the same as profits. They are the accumulation of undistributed profits over a period of time.)

And if you pay a dividend illegally – that is, it does not comply with your Memorandum and Articles of Association specification and you have insufficient profit reserves – the dividend will be treated as remuneration for the purposes of PAYE.

On the other hand, it is unwise to take no salary at all – this could eliminate you from the benefits of being within the UK social security system from which your state pension will be paid, as well as closing the opportunity to effective tax planning in relation to personal and company pension contributions.

So, along with what you pay, the how is equally important. Make sure you carefully check the procedures involved in dividend payment.

You will need to minute the fact that sufficient reserves exist. Don't forget that if there are dividends payable periodically rather than simply at the year's end, you may need interim accounts to validate this. This is important, particularly if you have an investigation by the H M Revenue & Customs (formerly the Inland Revenue and H M Customs & Excise), as they will be looking very carefully at the timings of the payments against your reserves at that time.

# 14. Information Consultation Directive

The way to get things done is not to mind who gets the credit for doing them.
**Benjamin Jowett, English scholar and master of Balliol College, Oxford**

The EU's Information Consultation Directive was effective from April 2005 for establishments with 150 or more staff members. It will come into force in 2007 for those with 100 plus, and in 2008 for those with 50 plus.

Regarded as the biggest change in corporate governance since the Second World War, this directive gives all employees working in establishments that employ more than 50 people the right to be informed and consulted, through their elected representative, on all matters affecting their job and employment prospects.

There will be enforcement penalties for non-compliance with this directive, thought to be in the region of a £75,000 'no tolerance' fine.

Although it is open to interpretation by EU member states, the general right to information and consultation covers the following:

1. Recent and probable developments relating to the activity and economic situation of the establishment

2. Situation, structure and probable development of employment and any anticipated measures envisaged, in particular where there is a threat to employment

3. Decisions that are likely to lead to substantial changes in work organisations, including redundancies and transfers of undertakings, such as the sale of your business.

Any information has to be provided well before decisions are taken. Consultation, which is defined as an exchange of views and the establishment of dialogue, must take place.

The elected employee representatives will naturally be bound by confidentiality provisions, although the actual policing of this will inevitably be very difficult.

## How it will work in practice

So how will employee representation be deemed to operate?

Although there is no need to have permanent information and consultation arrangements in place, it is likely that ad hoc ones will be rejected by the unions. There will be a minimum standard, however, which is likely to include a statutory fall-back framework for employees unwilling to introduce the necessary information and consultative framework.

The route to compliance will generally be the establishment of a works council or the appointment of a nominated employee representative to sit on your board. If 10 per cent or more of your company's employees request you to establish such a council or representative seat, you'll be required to do it.

In short, you may have a limited time to implement this directive. Or it may already be too late, depending on the size of your business. To get the most out of it, look at training and development for those staff who are likely to be involved so that they gain an understanding of their role and its implications.

By the way consultation does not mean agreement, but it does mean a two-way discussion – at least in theory!

# 15. Insider dealing

It is astonishing with how little wisdom mankind can be governed, when that little wisdom is its own.
**W. R. Inge, Anglican prelate and Professor of Divinity, Cambridge**

When boom or bust threatens, insider dealing scandals seem to hit the headlines. But what is this strange phenomenon?

Basically, insider dealing happens when someone who has inside information about the performance of a company – information which, it could be said, is not yet available to the market as a whole – buys or sells shares in that company. The prohibition applies to buying and selling during what's called the 'closed' period – the two-month period preceding the preliminary announcement of a company's annual or biannual result.

Disclosing price-sensitive information during the closed period also falls under the prohibition, even if done without any specific intent.

This is one example of the very strict regulations in place on how directors and employees conduct themselves when dealing in shares in their businesses. Most directors of listed companies are aware of these restrictions, but too few seem aware of their extent.

What if a director wants to play the market in what is essentially an open period? Even in this case, they would be well advised to seek clearance in advance from the company.

Note that the prohibitions apply whether or not the director has receipt of the confidential information, and that they also apply to what are called 'connected persons' – defined in the Companies Act, and including as a minimum the director's domestic partner and children.

Any breach of these guidelines could easily result in a disqualification and, potentially, criminal proceedings. These rules principally apply to public quoted companies. In privately owned companies, it is possible to pass a resolution to allow shares to be traded.

# 16. IR35 and independent contractors

Every problem has a gift for you in its hands.
**Richard Bach, American writer**

Are the people that work for you your employees or not? This seems like a very basic question. After all, if they are your employees, you deduct PAYE and NIC from their wages and pay contributions on their behalf; and if they aren't, you don't. Right?

Not quite. If only it were so simple, but sadly it isn't. Ultimately, only H M Revenue & Customs can verify an individual's employment status for tax purposes; but for employment law purposes, their status would be determined by an employment tribunal. And in the end, there could be two different results!

All this falls under the IR35, legislation introduced in 2000 by the former Inland Revenue to cover employee status.

No single factor will determine whether someone is employed or not. But clearly, the costs of getting it wrong can be enormous.

Imagine you have been utilising the services of a 'self-employed' part-time bookkeeper for some years. Eventually your requirements change and you now need bookkeeping help full time.

If it turns out that this person is actually classed as an employee, not only will you have been deemed to be paying them net (and you of course will be liable for the tax and NIC you should have collected from them), you will also owe employer's NIC and will potentially have to fund holiday pay arrears and sick pay. You could even be facing a redundancy or unfair dismissal situation – scary!

The H M Revenue & Customs is very interested indeed in this area, as they stand to lose out substantially. A few points to verify, therefore, are:

- Can the individual work when they choose?
- Do they use their own books and equipment, such as a computer?
- Can they work for several employers?
- Can they choose whether to accept the work or not?
- Do they accept some financial risk in their work?
- Can they send a substitute to carry out their work?
- Are they paid if off sick or on holiday?
- Do they raise an invoice?

These are the areas that an employment tribunal and the Inland Revenue will look at when assessing someone for status. You should also note that it is irrelevant whether the contractor sets up a company to provide the service or trades as a sole trader or partnership. The same principles apply in either case.

# 17. Money laundering

It is better that ten guilty escape than one innocent suffer.
**William Blackstone, English jurist and producer of the historical treatise on Common Law**

Money laundering – isn't that 'something to do with drink, drugs, prostitution and gambling'? You should be so lucky!

Have you ever been overpaid by a customer? Is that overpayment still sitting on your sales ledger? Or have you taken it into profit? If so, you could be **guilty** of money laundering under the Money Laundering and Proceeds of Crime Act 2002, which was updated in 2003 and is now in force. And if you are, you and your company could face very serious litigation, leading to severe penalties including imprisonment.

So if you've been overpaid, you need to look into whether you have attempted to repay that customer – and I mean persistent efforts. Again, if you haven't tried, you could be deemed **guilty** of money laundering.

What's even more interesting in this situation is the position of your auditors.

Under the new legislation, auditors must appoint a senior member of their organisation to act as a money laundering reporting officer (MLRO). This MLRO has to make decisions as to whether, on completing their standard audit work and discovering, say, an overpayment, they need to report the act.

Even more interesting is the fact that if they do make this decision, they will not be letting you know of their intention. This would be classed as 'tipping off' – an action that would in turn incriminate them!

You could therefore find yourself being prosecuted for having a balance on a ledger that goes back some time, even though you may simply have forgotten it's there. And your auditors can't remind you about it!

## Staying out of trouble

The implications of these regulations are wide-ranging. You could get into trouble for any comment, even made in jest, about non-declaration of all income, for instance, or the paying of personal invoices with corporate funds without proper allocation to direction loans (monies the director borrows from the company). If your auditor heard of this, they would feel legally bound to report the matter – without giving you the chance of correcting the situation.

Penalties for money laundering are severe. They can include imprisonment and disqualification of your director status.

The regulations are still relatively new, and there are bound to be a number of test cases to establish principles. So make sure you aren't one of them by talking in broad terms with your auditors well in advance of your next audit, and then taking appropriate action.

Your solicitor and other professional advisers are subject to similar rules.

Also, if you handle large cash sums you must register under these new rules, as you need to be able to prove that you took appropriate steps to confirm that the funds given to you were 'clean'. This means taking such action as obtaining a certified copy of a passport or driving licence and a utility bill to prove the person giving you the funds is actually who they claim they are.

# 18. 'Passing off'

Today, if you are not confused, you are just not thinking clearly.
**U. Peter, author**

As you know, as long as you've registered your company at Companies House, other companies can't use its name. And if you've registered your trademark, your brand can't be plagiarised. But what can you do if someone presents their goods as yours and you have no trademark protection?

Your action would come under the old common-law tort (meaning injury or wrong) of 'passing off'. In order to succeed in obtaining an injunction for this, you need to prove the following:

1.  There was a misrepresentation.

2.  It was made by a competitor as part of plying their trade.

3.  This misrepresentation was made to potential customers with the calculated intent of damaging your business and goodwill.

4.  Actual damage was caused to your business.

The key is to be able to demonstrate damage and intent to damage. Customer confusion is unfortunately not enough.

Recent case law, however, has added a further dimension by identifying fraudsters known as 'cybersquatters'. Essentially, these are individuals or companies who carry out an activity with the sole purpose of using it dishonestly in the future. For example, registering a domain name with the sole intent of selling it to another so that the buyer can use it dishonestly.

This means that goodwill is protectable, even though the offence hasn't actually occurred; and that those people or entities that merely threaten to commit the action will be liable.

Of course, the best defence is being prepared. So register your brand: any infringement is then much clearer in terms of bringing an action.

# 19. Registered office

Hell hath no fury like a bureaucrat scorned.
**Milton Friedman, US economist and advocate of Laissez-faire Capitalism**

Every business has to have a registered office, and the 1985 Companies Act states that its address must be on all correspondence. This is the address where all the company's records are kept and where official mail is sent.

You'll need to bear a few issues in mind here. This address will determine where your tax affairs will be dealt with and where, for instance, summonses are served. So if you're a small company owner/director working from home, you may prefer not to designate your own house as the registered office.

As you cannot use a post office box, you may wish to use the office of your solicitors or accountants; for Scottish registered companies, the registered office must be within Scotland. These services are readily available for a fairly moderate sum, usually as little as £100. Although you cannot, of course, trade from this address, it does formalise an area of your business and gives you one less concern!

# 20. Stakeholder pensions

It is sad to grow old but nice to ripen.
**Brigitte Bardot**

Everyone, but everyone, is aware of the pension timebomb now. And to help manage this precarious situation, the government introduced the stakeholder pension scheme in October 2001.

The essence of this legislation is to ensure that **all** employers who employ more than five people provide a facility to deduct pension contributions direct from the payroll, or alternatively provide a substitute scheme. This scheme must be approved by H M Revenue & Customs – and don't just assume yours will be.

You do not, as an employer, have to contribute to this scheme, though many employers do. But you must have a scheme and, specifically, it has got to be a money purchase scheme. Management charges can't be more than 1 per cent, and the minimum contribution can't be higher than £20.

If you do not comply, be warned you will face prosecution as a director, and both personal and corporate fines.

# 21. Substantial property transactions

Property is organised robbery.
**George Bernard Shaw**

Have you ever bought or considered buying an asset from your company, such as a car or a building or even a debtor? Well, **don't**, at least not without getting advice, as otherwise you may well be breaking the law.

Generally directors (including shadow directors[1]) are prevented from entering into substantial property transactions. Note, however, that the word 'substantial' is somewhat misleading. It is legally defined as the lower of £100,000 or 10 per cent of the company's net assets (less than £2,000 is not relevant). So if your assets are, say, £50,000 and you buy your car back from the company at a cost of £20,000, you would be breaking the law!

This issue can be managed by gaining approval from the

[1] See Structure, section 17, p. 37

company itself, however. You can do this during a shareholder meeting by way of an ordinary resolution – a simple majority vote in favour.

These rules also apply to persons legally connected with the director concerned (spouse or domestic partner and any children), or any company in which they have more than a 20 per cent shareholding.

If you don't follow these procedures, the company can cause the contract to be voided. This could create a damages claim, so please take advice before you act.

# People and personal liabilities: the human factor

> Most people ... find a disorientating mismatch between the long-term nature of their liabilities and the increasingly short-term nature of their assets.
> **James A. Baldwin, American novelist and playwright**

More than ever before, your personal liabilities are in the legal spotlight. 'Trial by tabloid' has become commonplace.

For some people, it seems that bringing a litigious action against a company or their employer reaps greater rewards than actually working. There have been large payouts and an increasing number of substantial sentences, as well as very hefty personal fines, inflicted on the business community.

## A bitter pill ...

Of course, many claimants are highly justified in bringing an action against a company. But if you suddenly find yourself falling foul of the law because you were unaware of a particular regulation, any subsequent action against your company can be a trial indeed. And where you have shouldered this liability because of a colleague's inadequacy or negligence, the pill can be a very bitter one.

In addition to any unpalatable fines or prison sentences that might be doled out, there's a further penalty: a successful case against you will almost certainly mean you'll be disqualified from acting in a company as a director, sometimes for up to 15 years.

Ultimately it will always be **your** problem. Over 30 per cent of disqualifications are for the maximum 15 years, making it very difficult for you to manage any business for a very long time indeed. That will almost certainly affect your personal credit rating indefinitely.

To manage any potential liability, advice at an early stage is critical, and of course it must be the right type of advice. Seek out people with practical, relevant, hands-on support. Remember that however good your case, you will need to have complete confidence in your adviser, and that it's also essential never to take your eyes off your business generally.

## Be prepared

Prevention is, however, the only real medicine and systems, systems, systems, will help enormously. By that I mean sound, comprehensive, reliable management information.

The use of non-executive directors to support your board can be very valuable if you choose the right person or persons. Their 'been there, done that' knowledge can put the mechanisms in place that will help with basic compliance principles.

I would also recommend that you proceed to enlighten both yourself and your top team regarding the ins and outs of compliance. Because of the shared liability issue, a mutual understanding will support the organisation.

Free or low-cost update seminars are available from a number of providers, both specialists and the legal profession generally. Make the most of this by ensuring that you attend as many of them as you can.

Finally, appoint a first-class accountant and solicitor. You need to be able to communicate well with them, and to ensure they can relate to your business and to any issues and concerns it has about liability.

# 1. Alternative dispute resolution

Informed decision-making comes from a long tradition of guessing and then blaming others for inadequate results.
**Scott Adams, creator of Dilbert comic strip**

Legal costs are generally high, and you can easily find already substantial expenses escalating out of control – sadly, very often to no avail. So it makes sense to avoid litigation if at all possible. Alternative dispute resolution (ADR) provides such a route to settling civil disputes.

ADR is being used more and more not only because it is often cheaper than a court trial, but also because it's speedier. In fact, the courts themselves are keen to push parties towards ADR to help manage the substantial litigation backlogs they must contend with.

It is not possible to force any litigants into using ADR unless it is a condition of a contract (a good idea if you wish this process to be adhered to in the first instance), but the courts do take a dim view of litigants who unreasonably refuse to at least attempt ADR.

## ADR procedures

Various methods of ADR exist, including the long-established ombudsman scheme, plus mediation, arbitration and a number of less widely known procedures. Each applies to different legal issues.

Arbitration is one of the more established ADR procedures. It is based on the parties referring their issue to a third party. If a travel agency, say, is one of the parties, the third party might be the Association of British Travel Agents (ABTA). This third party then creates a legally binding contract to obtain a fair resolution of the dispute, which can then be enforced by the courts, subject to any anti-public policy clauses. This contract or agreement is arrived at via an arbitration tribunal. Arbitration thus provides a private, informal and cost-effective procedure involving little recourse to appeal.

Mediation is significantly different. The mediator will not make a decision; rather, the idea is that the parties involved will make a decision (hopefully!). So, unlike arbitration, it allows for a direct route to court if no agreement can be reached.

Conciliation is similar in a number of ways to mediation, but the mediator is more interventionist. Their primary goal is to conciliate, mostly by seeking concessions from both parties.

There are other methods: expert determination (where the neutral third party is chosen on the basis of special qualifications, and then determines the outcome); neutral evaluation (not mediation, but a frank appraisal of a case's legal merits); and Med-Arb (a mix of mediation and arbitration). All provide a route for exploring a settlement without recourse to court. You just need to find the one tailored to both parties' needs.

The key is to attempt ADR as part of a dispute process. It can save you time, money and considerable heartache.

# 2. Compromise agreements

*Illegitimis non carborundum* (Latin for 'Don't let the bastards grind you down').
**General Joseph Stilwell, United States Army 4\* General**

You are never given a wish without also being given the power to make it come true. You may have to work for it, however.
**Richard Bach, American writer**

Because of the cost, time and worry that undoubtedly form part of any litigious action relating to employment, you need to seriously consider solutions that sidestep claims in the first place. These are known as compromise agreements.

Although nothing can provide absolute certainty, provided a compromise agreement has been drawn up in the appropriate manner, it's as near to that state as you are likely to get.

The agreement is legally binding on the parties as long as the employee concerned has taken independent advice (which, incidentally, you must pay for). It effectively creates a full and final settlement by providing that the employee will not bring an action, such as unfair dismissal.

The agreement can provide for other issues, including payments in lieu and severance pay, for example.

Don't expect the agreement to be brief: it could easily extend to several pages. It will cover such matters as the specific compensation offered and accepted and the detailed terms on which this has been provided. There is usually also a confidentiality clause.

If you happen to be the recipient of such an agreement, you may want to negotiate the inclusion of a reference **and** its contents. That way, you can ensure that any reference to your skills, abilities and so on will be more accurate, as this description will have been part of the negotiation process.

# 3. Cooling off

When you go to buy use your eyes, not your ears.
**Czech proverb**

Life is short, the art long, opportunity fleeting,
experiment treacherous, judgment difficult.
**Hippocrates**

'Cooling off', which refers to a change of mind, is a measure that protects the consumer in a contractual relationship by allowing them to back out of the contract during a designated period after signing.

As a contract needs no signature, the smallest of transactions – even purchasing a pint of milk from your local milkman – can be said to be a contract. So where transactions of any kind take place, and contracts rear their heads, caution has to be the name of the game.

The Consumer Credit Act states that for a cooling off period to be legitimate in a contract, the main requirements are as follows:

1. Credit must be involved.

2. The contract needs to have been signed on the trade premises.

3. Some sort of face-to-face negotiations need to have taken place between buyer and seller.

A typical transaction covered under this Act would be buying a car under a hire purchase agreement. In these circumstances the consumer has five days to reverse their decision.

## Other consumer protection acts

There are, of course, numerous other pieces of legislation protecting the consumer. The Consumer Protection (Distance

Selling) Regulations 2000 covers the kind of transactions carried out online, for instance. Under this statute, once you receive the goods you have a seven-day cooling off period, and if you have not been informed of this right to cancel in the supplier's terms and conditions, this period could be extended by a further three months.

From the vendor's point of view, if a consumer requests a refund under these terms – and this must be in writing – you have 30 days to return the payment. There is an option to charge the consumer for any costs incurred in the return of the goods. The person acquiring the goods is not actually obliged to return them, but rather only to make them available for return – a point that needs to be taken into account.

Timeshares have their own specific piece of legislation – the Timeshare Act 1992 – which allows a 14-day cooling off period if the agreement is signed in the UK, and a ten-day cooling off period if signed elsewhere in the EU.

Finally, there are specific regulations related to transactions carried out off site. Provided the transaction value exceeds £35 and the sales call was unsolicited, a seven-day cooling off period will apply. This would typically cover door-to-door sales calls.

None of these regulations apply to business to business transactions. It is all legislation to protect the consumer, as I've indicated. However, if you are in the business of selling something to the consumer market, these are the areas that need handling in an appropriate manner.

# 4. Corporate manslaughter and corporate killing

In no sense do I advocate evading or defying the law ...
that would lead to anarchy. An individual who breaks a
law that his conscience tells him is unjust, and who
willingly accepts the penalty of imprisonment in order to
arouse the conscience of the community over its
injustice, is in reality expressing the highest respect for
the law.
**Martin Luther King, Jr**

Corporate manslaughter is an old established principle based in common law. It is defined as an instance where activities managed by an individual in the company who is 'the controlling or directing mind' of the business lead to the death of a person or person through gross negligence.

Needless to say, this is very difficult to prove, particularly in larger companies, and to date only a handful of cases have been successful.

In the UK there has been widespread concern over the existing law, which many feel has failed to protect the public just as they are beset by a number of catastrophes, notably in the rail industry. The government has reviewed the law, particularly the problematic element of pinpointing a senior manager guilty of gross negligence, and is now planning to introduce a new offence: corporate killing.

While this isn't on the statute books yet, it is believed to be imminent.

There are several principles to this new offence, as proposed by the Law Commission. It will broadly look like the individual offence of killing by gross negligence. It will also occur if the organisation concerned acted in a less than reasonable manner.

However, whereas for a successful individual action you would

121

need to prove that the risk was obvious, no such proof will be necessary for a corporate claim. In addition, any death will be regarded as having been caused by the management's failure; and this inevitably means that the way an organisation manages its responsibilities for health and safety[*1] is paramount. Even more so, because any failure in maintaining appropriate health and safety regulations will be regarded as the cause of death, even if the immediate cause is actually the act or indeed the omission to act of an individual.

These penalties apply equally to the board of directors as much as to the company itself. That means you personally could go to jail if found guilty. Keep your health and safety monitoring up to scratch, and acquaint yourself with the new law when it is published.

To keep a check on the progress of this law, refer to the Department of Trade and Industry website (www.dti.gov.uk).

# 5. Directors' duty of care and skill

Asked what his secret was for lasting so long and being so successful as the president of the University of Michigan, Dr James R. Angell explained: 'Grow antennae, not horns.'
**Dr Douglas Southall Freeman, American journalist and author**

One of the fundamental principles of a director's duty, as enshrined in common law, is that they must act with care and skill. The problem is to determine how careful is careful and how skilful is skilful.

[*1] See Compliance, section 11, p. 98

Principally, case law says that a director need not have any greater degree of skill than would reasonably be expected from a person with his knowledge and experience. That in itself means there is no single professional standard for company directors. So the standard varies according to a director's function and the amount of time they are required to spend on their duties.

To a large extent, therefore, this is a subjective test and case law would certainly say that a mere error of judgment would not constitute a breach of duty.

However, case law continues to increase the level of care and skill necessary to discharge this duty. The Barings Bank case, where a chief trader's actions bankrupted a venerable organisation, confirmed that directors have a duty to ensure they have sufficient knowledge of the company's activities to ensure they can properly discharge their duties.

Can you read a balance sheet? If not, it's possible that you may not be acting with sufficient care and skill. Should your business fail a liquidator may feel they have a good case to bring a contribution order against you – which means you would have to contribute to a shortfall in outstanding creditor moneys.

# 6. Fiduciary responsibilities

An ounce of prevention is worth a pound of cure.
**Henry de Bracton, *De Legibus* (1240)**

Along with a director's duty of care and skill,[1] the other common law principle concerning their behaviour is fiduciary responsibilities.

Fiduciary means 'to care for and protect'. It applies to directors because they are also trustees of their companies' assets, and thus have a responsibility to care for and protect them.

[1] See People and personal liabilities, section 5, p. 122

123

A director's fiduciary responsibilities are to:
- Act in good faith in the interests of the company
- Exercise their power only for a proper purpose and not to enter into a position of conflict.

Because a director's principal duty of care belongs to the company, and because – by virtue of their position – they have access to valuable information, a director is not allowed to act in such a way that his own interests conflict with that of the company.

In one recent case, a director purchased commercial property which his company had neither the wherewithal nor the intention of buying. He had gone ahead with the transaction without the company's approval – and ended up having to recompense it.

## Practicalities of protection

Disclosure of a possible conflict and approval to carry out a transaction must be obtained from the shareholders in a general meeting.

Be wary, also, of selling company assets at less than their real value, unless this can be clearly demonstrated to be for the benefit of the company. Likewise, diverting a contract from your company to another business in which you have an interest could be classed as a breach of your fiduciary duty.

As a director cannot benefit at the expense of his company unless the company gives its permission, be vigilant in the process of awarding directors bonuses and remuneration packages.

In one company, the sole director and shareholder had to repay his end-of-year bonus to the new owners of his business after it was sold, as he had no company permission for the payment. It is quite a difficult task for a sole owner/director to get permission, but it's one which the law lords in this case said was, nevertheless, a requirement.

The essence of acting properly is, as one judge said, 'to act with sunshine' – meaning to act with honesty and openness in all that you do. Ensure that you declare any possible conflicts of interest, and remember that this includes associated persons. Act impartially: don't vote personally on these issues, or you could make a potentially expensive mistake!

# 7. Liability for directors on winding up

The real measure of your wealth is how much you'd be worth if you lost all your money.
**Anon**

When corporate insolvency hits – that is, you find yourself unable to pay your debts as they become due or have a greater amount of liabilities than assets – your next task is winding up your business. This means settling your accounts and liquidating the assets so you can distribute net proceeds to shareholders and get on with dissolving the company.

But you need to be vigilant before the fact. If you even begin to suspect that your company may become insolvent, speed is of the essence: you will need to get advice fast, and act very swiftly indeed.

Any insolvency is managed by a specific department within the Department of Trade and Industry, known as the Insolvency Service. This service, which is delivered through official receivers (OR), private administrators and insolvency practitioners, investigates both individuals and companies that are in liquidation.

The job of these people is to establish the reasons behind the insolvency and report on the individuals concerned.

Liquidation can be triggered by a number of different events involving both partnerships and companies. Whatever the reason, the first step is often a compulsory winding up. The action is usually started by a court order which, when presented to the court, states that the business owes money and that it is unable to make the payment.

The business is then moved into compulsory liquidation. At this point the OR become involved in the process, their job being to inform creditors and shareholders of the imminent winding up, and whether there are sufficient assets available for distribution. A liquidator will then be appointed to realise the assets and make an appropriate distribution to creditors.

## Where the director comes in

Your position as a director in these proceedings needs careful consideration. It is important to note that the term 'director' applies to all directors, even those who don't hold the official title of director (such as shadow directors[*1]).

All directors have a duty to understand the financial position of their business, and the OR have the legal right to interview all directors immediately when a winding-up order is made. So you'll need to be ready and waiting.

If the OR do not interview you immediately, they will interview you later, and require you to complete a questionnaire sent out in advance. You have a legal requirement to cooperate and supply any and all information related to the claim that the OR deem necessary. Refusal to cooperate is seen to be contempt of court, which carries both penal and financial penalties.

Once this process has finished, the OR, liquidator or receiver has a duty to send a report on the conduct and behaviour of all directors (including shadow directors) who have held office in the business during the last three years of trading. The Secretary of State then has to make a decision as to whether or not it is in the public's interest to seek to disqualify the director. Typical reasons include, but not exclusively, the following:

[*1] See Structure, section 17, p. 39

- Failure to keep proper accounting records
- Continuing to trade an insolvent business
- Failure to prepare and file accounts or returns to Companies House
- Failure to pay tax that is due.

## The penalties

If, as a result of this report, proceedings are commenced for the disqualification of a director and the court decides that this is appropriate, the disqualification will last for a minimum period of two years up to a maximum of 15 years. On top of this the director may be deemed to have criminal and personal liability for fraudulent trading and/or wrongful trading, if relevant.

In addition, a director of an insolvent business cannot, for a five-year period after winding up, be involved in another company using a name that is so similar to the failed company's that it suggests an association with the failed company – unless the other company was in existence for at least 12 months prior to the insolvency.

As ever, prevention is the best course of action.

Take advice as soon as possible from a professional. It can be useful to contact the UK Insolvency Helpline on 0800 074 6918 (or see their website at www.insolvencyhelpline.co.uk). Carefully monitor the financial prospects of the company using budgets and forecasts, and do whatever is practical to cut costs and reduce risk. If in doubt at all about your personal position, take advice at the earliest stage: this is the right thing to do and you'll always be seen as having acted properly.

And here's an inside tip – keep verbatim minutes of these meetings. They are an excellent source of evidence!

# 8. Limited partnerships

> There are no shortcuts to any place worth going.
> **Anon**

Setting up a business as a partnership is fraught with problems of liability. By law, a partner is personally liable – even down to the clothes on his back – for any liabilities the partnership takes on. And this is a joint and several liability, which means that a group of partners are liable for each other.

## Halfway house

One way of approaching a partnership is to opt for what's called a limited partnership (not to be confused with a limited liability partnership or LLP, which is described below). This is a sort of halfway house between a company and a partnership in that, other than the designated partner (the so-called general partner – there must be at least one), the liability for the other partners is limited to the amount they have invested in the business.

Unlike an ordinary partnership, a limited partnership must register at Companies House.

A limited partner must not take part in the management of the business. If they do so, the benefit of limited liability is lost.

## Limited liability partnership

The LLP is a fairly new business entity, but since its inception a substantial number of professional practices have set up in this format in an effort to reduce risk and limit liability.

Like a limited partnership, an LLP must register at Companies House. It must nominate at least two members, known as the 'designated members', who are responsible for ensuring statutory compliance.

The LLP is a separate legal entity and can therefore raise money and grant charges in a way in which an ordinary partnership cannot. It must file accounts at Companies House, but its members are taxed as if the LLP was an ordinary partnership.

The LLP must have an incorporation document (similar to a partnership agreement), but this does not have to be registered at Companies House and is not a public document. It can submit abbreviated accounts if its turnover levels and so on are applicable.

Either natural or legal personnel can be members of an LLP and are subject to disqualification related to their behaviour, just as company directors are.

So why have an LLP rather than a regular partnership? It's mostly down to managing risk and creating a flexible entity that can be used to fund growth. However, the loss of privacy that results from publishing accounts in the public domain has to be considered as a major disadvantage for some businesses.

# 9. Preferential payments

The buck stops with the guy who signs the cheques.
**Rupert Murdoch**

As its name indicates, a preferential payment involves paying one creditor in preference to another. Although by no means unusual, the practice of making preferential payments in the day-to-day management of your business, particularly in an impending insolvency situation, is fraught with danger.

When insolvency looms, instinct kicks in and survival is uppermost in your mind, it can seem very appealing to first pay off the creditors most likely to either provide essential goods or services or the one who has a priority personal charge against your own assets in the event of failure. It is not, however, legal – and indeed such actions could cause the directors even more problems.

In a situation of impending insolvency, the job of the company director is to protect the creditors first and to treat them all fairly and equally. Any payment made outside this arena can be seized by the insolvency practitioner and added back into the pot of total funds available for distribution. If it isn't possible to retrieve these funds for whatever reason, you, as director, may find you will need to make up the shortfall!

From the creditors' point of view, it is essential to keep accurate financial records of the pattern of payments received over a given period. Any such information needs to be complete and accurate and must identify payments made against specific invoices. So if, for example, you often receive payment before your standard terms of credit, claims for preferential treatment are going to be much harder to substantiate.

# 10. Trading while disqualified

> The world at large does not judge us by who we are and what we know; it judges us by what we have.
> **Joyce Brothers, family psychologist and advice columnist**

Currently, some 2,000 plus directors are disqualified each year. The disqualification is handed out by the Secretary of State for Trade and Industry, and will last for a period of between two and 15 years.

Examples of reasons for disqualification are:

- Continuing to trade at a time when their company was insolvent
- Failure to keep proper accounting records
- Failure to prepare and file accounts or make returns to Companies House

• Failure to return or pay over to the crown any tax which is due.

What is perhaps a real concern is that if you continue to act as a director once you have been disqualified (and don't forget that this includes acting as a shadow director[*1]), not only will you be committing a criminal offence, but you could also be personally liable for all the debts the company incurred since your disqualification.

You can do a search on who has been disqualified on the Companies House Disqualified Directors Register, which is in the public domain; the website address is www.companieshouse.gov.uk/ddir/, or you can call their hotline at 0845 601 3540.

What is also worrying is that the whole board may find themselves liable. Have you checked out who is and isn't disqualified on your team (not just registered directors)?

One case I recall went as follows.

Mr Shifty was disqualified after he allowed his business to continue to trade whilst insolvent. Shortly afterwards, he established a new business in which he appointed his wife as sole owner/director. This was in fact a sham: his wife had nothing to do with the running or management of the company. The courts ordered that both he and his wife were personally liable for the debts of the new company when this later failed – and on top of that, Mr Shifty faced a two-year prison sentence.

[*1] See Structure, section 17, p. 39

# 11. Types of directors and non-executives

> If the profession you have chosen has some unexpected inconveniences, console yourself that no profession is without them, and that all the perplexities of business are softness compared with the vacancy of idleness.
> **Samuel Johnson**

It is possible to hold the title of director without being registered at Companies House. In fact, it's possible to give an individual director status and potentially all the liabilities associated with this role simply by giving them the title of director.

It isn't at all unusual to give out such titles without any intention of giving the individual director authority or even liability. But unfortunately, the law doesn't necessarily see it that way.

Let's say you give your sales representative a business card describing them as a sales director. Then, when they carry out a transaction on the basis of this identity, they are potentially seen in law to be acting as a company director.

The test (like so many legal tests!) is one of reasonableness. Was it reasonable for the other parties involved in the transaction to believe that they were dealing with a board-appointed director? If the answer is yes, then in all probability, in the eyes of the law, they were! But not only does this give rise to all sorts of potential personal liabilities for the individual. Almost certainly it will give rise to some corporate issues.

So you need to exercise caution. In some industries, such as advertising and the media, it is the norm to give out such titles. But be careful, as you could be handing out what looks like a prestigious title, only to have it backfire in all sorts of ways.

# Alternate, nominee and non-executive directors

Alternate directors are those individuals who stand in place of an absent director, provided such a facility is allowable in the company's Memorandum and Articles of Association. And these directors, like their colleagues, could be letting themselves in for a number of personal risks if litigation is brought against the board for decisions in which they participated. So pick up this particular mantle only after some very serious consideration.

A nominee director is someone nominated to the board to represent the interests of a particular stakeholder group. The important word here is **represent**. This does not in any way change their principal duty of care, which still belongs to the company (at least in theory!).

Finally there's the non-executive director. This type differs from the executive director not only by virtue of the fact that they have no management function but also because of their time commitment to the business, which is usually much more limited than an executive director's. These people are usually not employees and are remunerated either as a self-employed person or via another corporate vehicle.

As liability is usually joint and several [1] for all directors, all directors of whatever substance (whether executive or non-executive) will potentially share liability.

[1] See Funding, section 11, p. 67

# 12. Unfair dismissal

The thing that really worries businesses today is the great number of people still on their payroll who are unemployed.
**Lily Tomlin, US actress and comedienne**

Once someone has been an employee for more than 12 months, and provided they are under 65 (or whatever the normal retirement age is with the organisation), dismissal becomes very difficult. In fact, employees have rights in common law for wrongful dismissal from the moment the employment begins – one example is breach of contract – and in these cases the whole of the loss is recoverable without limit.

The basic rule under employment law is that a company needs to establish a fair reason for dismissal.

Some reasons are automatically unfair, such as pregnancy, childbirth, membership of unions, a refusal to work on Sundays (though the latter only applies to employees who joined after 26 August 2004), or a case arising from a transfer of a business's assets. Potentially fair reasons include lack of qualifications, misconduct, incompetence and redundancy.

What is important to remember is that it is the employer who must prove the reason, and then act reasonably. From October 2004 some statutory disciplinary and dismissal procedures have been in place, and it is essential that you adhere to these at the very least, or the dismissal could be deemed automatically unfair. These rules apply to all employers, regardless of how many people they actually employ.

## How to get it right

To dismiss someone fairly you must follow a three-step procedure. Start with a letter that provides information on the reasons for the actions. Follow with a face-to-face meeting (allowing enough time for the employee to consider the issues), during which the employee can be accompanied by a colleague or union representative. Finally, hold a meeting to announce the decision. This series of meetings may be extended if the employee then appeals.

Employers should also be wary of a constructive dismissal. This happens when life has been made so difficult for the employee that they feel they can no longer remain in the job, and must resign. In these cases the resignation is counted as dismissal by the employer. In many cases, this dismissal will be regarded as unfair, but the facts of each case will need individual consideration. The areas likely to be included are:

• Changing job terms and conditions without consultation
• Demotion and failure to provide support.

Recent case law has also shown that not managing workplace stress can be classed as constructive dismissal. The key is procedure, procedure, procedure, as well as the maintenance of comprehensive personnel records. As an employer, the burden of proof rests with you, and you need evidence!

# 13. Vicarious liability

> When you reach the end of your rope, tie a knot in it and hang on.
> **Thomas Jefferson**

When you employ people, you become responsible for any consequences of their actions during the course of their employment or work time. The bottom line is that if they do not behave in an appropriate manner, it is the employer who may be prosecuted for the employee's actions!

If your employee commits an offence, you may also have to compensate the victim – even if the criminal action is only incidentally related to the employee's duties. So for instance, if your manager who handles clients retains funds belonging to a customer with intent to make them his own property, your company will have to compensate the victim for the fraud of your employee!

You can take fidelity insurance to guard against such a risk – but have you actually done that? How would you insure against your manager assaulting your secretary? And would you be liable anyway?

The answer is that if it can be argued that there is a connection between the employee's actions and the duties which the employee is carrying out, there will be a civil liability for the employer.

The most likely employers to be affected by this law employ people in a position of trust towards others, such as nursing and care homes, or housing associations and charities.

And yes, you can insure; but check your current policy, as many have exclusions for criminal acts. What is clear is that you will be responsible for the actions of your employees in relevant circumstances, whether or not you authorised them. Your main defence is that the employee was not negligent – that is, they were reasonably careful or were acting in their own right rather than the employer's business.

A key issue relates to employees who drive on the job. Companies have a very specific duty to ensure that employees comply with road safety issues, such as road worthiness and safe operation of the vehicle. You must carry out risk assessments on vehicles including road worthiness tyres, the MOT and so on. A failure to comply will mean severe penalties, including unlimited financial liability and prison. And these will apply to the company and even individual directors if there is a direct link of responsibility to that person.

# 14. Wrongful v. fraudulent trading

So you think that money is the root of all evil. Have you ever asked what is the root of all money?
**Ayn Rand, Russian-born screenwriter**

## Wrongful trading

Directors (including shadow directors[*1]) who continue to trade after their business has gone into insolvent liquidation are committing a civil offence known as wrongful trading. The Insolvency Act 2000 states that a director should have ceased to trade when they knew or ought to have known that the business could not pay its debts as they became due.

Corporate funders will often raise wrongful trading as an issue in investment agreements – which is a good reason indeed why all directors should monitor their financial performance at all times.

The test applied is to ask whether the person in question acted with the skills, knowledge and experience of a reasonably diligent person. This implies, quite rightly, that different people are required to act in different ways. Finance people will not be expected to act with the same portfolio of skills, for example, as sales personnel – and vice versa.

The penalty for wrongful trading, if successfully brought about, is a contribution order – a requirement to contribute personally to creditor shortfalls – and that is a very serious issue. The director can also be disqualified.

Prevention is an obvious course of action. The key is to act in good faith at all times and manage risk. This includes ensuring you are conversant with the financial affairs of your business (ideally comparing budgets to actual performance at the very least!) and maintaining clear and proper accounting records. It is

[*1] See Structure, section 17, p. 39

also imperative that you keep written records such as minutes of key commercial decisions. Evidence of acting reasonably throughout a process is hugely important.

## Fraudulent trading

Wrongful trading is clearly not to be viewed lightly, but fraudulent trading is very serious indeed. It is a criminal offence that, if proven, will lead to automatic disqualification as a director at the very least, and possibly imprisonment.

Fraudulent trading means trading with an intent to defraud creditors, by actually knowing that there is no money available to pay for the goods or services they have ordered. The allegations for it require proof beyond reasonable doubt that there was intention to do so, and because of this requirement, litigious actions often fail. It is, however, absolutely essential that as soon as you become aware of any possible insolvency, you must cease trading. If you don't, it is quite possible that you could be perceived as trading with a specific intention to defraud.

# 15. Your name on a contract v. company name

I was taught very early that I would have to depend entirely upon myself; that my future lay in my own hands.
**Darius Ogden Mills, American banker**

How do you sign your letters, contracts, purchase requests and so on? It's important, as it must always be clear who is contracting with who.

Signing anything in your own name could increase the chances of a personal action against you as an individual, if there is cause for litigation at a later stage. So why not remove that possibility?

To be as certain as anyone can be about the contracting parties, ensure that all correspondence is signed using your functional title, such as sales director or managing director, and be absolutely certain to include the words 'for and on behalf of' your company, which should be named. Insert all this on electronic correspondence as well, including emails.

By signing your correspondence in this manner, it makes it quite clear to the other parties that you are not acting personally but as an agent of your company or business. This will hopefully eliminate any potential for personal litigation. So just do it!

# Management:
# taking care of business

A man is known by the company he organises.
**Ambrose Bierce, 19th Century American short story writer and journalist**

So many of us are so busy simply getting things done that it's all too easy for management to get lost in the shuffle. But there's no doubt that strong, sound management can hugely improve your business.

The trouble is always one of time. Resources have been diluted to such a degree that the hands-on approach has become a way of life for many business owners, leaving them little or no time for the actual management of the organisation. This in turn leads to decisions made in haste and often in error.

Then there are the many entrepreneurs drawn into their industry by a love of their product or service. They would find a hands-off approach alien, but if their businesses succeed, they may find they have less and less time for management, and may delegate to the unable. This can lead not just to frustration, but a failed venture.

It doesn't have to be this way. Modern technology has made available a whole raft of techniques and products that can render the management process so much easier and more efficient. And this has the added benefit of freeing up valuable time.

## Getting the right support

This section is no guide to management technique. Rather, it's a guide to support techniques and possible pitfalls. Management 'how to' books abound and there is inevitably one that will suit your personal style and type of business.

There is also a vast amount of training on offer, much of which is supported by subsidised funding. The Department of Trade and Industry's Business Link can be a valuable source of contacts (see their website at www.businesslink.gov.uk, or call them at 0845 600 9 006). If you don't ask, you won't get!

The key to good management, like so much in relation to liabilities and compliance, is good communication. If your team – never mind your outside support network of funders and advisers – is unaware of your intentions, you won't be able to make this happen, and your business could suffer.

# 1. Bank check software

One of the hardest things to teach our children about money matters is that it does.
**William Randolph Hearst, American newspaper magnate**

The banks make mistakes: directors are negligent.
**From the Chartered Institute of Taxation website**

Banks are a huge part of business life, so it's essential to ensure that you're on to a winner. But the fact is that banks often – in some cases very often – make mistakes, and sometimes overcharge you sums that are too large for comfort.

Don't ever forget: a bank is a business, and its business is based around lending money against which it makes charges. Those charges include interest and costs related to the management of your money, from processing cheques to paying standing orders and direct debits.

Although you (hopefully) will have negotiated your charges and interest costs with your bank, it is very difficult indeed to check that you are paying the correct sums each month or quarter or however often you are charged.

> One case I recall involved a small market gardener who had continued to pay interest at the penalty rate (the rate applied if he exceeded his agreed facility – an astonishing 30 per cent) on all his facilities, even when he had brought his account within his credit limit for nearly 12 months!
>
> This was only discovered by accident, when he had got his advisers to check his viability on trading in the future.

The good news is that specialist software is now available to help you calculate what the costs should be. It's available on the web or even via your auditors for a very modest cost – less than £50.

With this software, you enter your bank balances into the system against your agreed facility costs. If the results tell you you are being overcharged, then you will have evidence to help prove your case. You will need to ensure you have kept as much information as possible.

Here's a quick tip. Add up all the balances on your bank statement and take a mean average in a quarter; multiply this by the investment rate and divide by four. If you get the same as you are being charged approximately, then you are probably being charged correctly. If not, seek help.

Get on the web. As a starter, try ChargeChecker (see www.chargechecker.co.uk).

# 2. Board meeting basics

Bore, n: A person who talks when you wish him to listen.
**Ambrose Bierce, 19th Century American short story writer and journalist**

One of the symptoms of an approaching nervous break-down is the belief that one's work is terribly important.
**Bertrand Russell**

There are two things that can make a good board meeting a great one:

1. A capable chairman
2. A challenging agenda.

Although the law only requires you to have one board meeting a year to comply with the regulations, that won't be enough to really boost your company's performance.

The corporate governance section[*1] of this book provides more insight into the content of a board meeting, but here are a few practical tips.

Most board meetings in SMEs (small to medium-sized enterprises) are actually management meetings where members spend far too much time on operational issues. (These definitely need to be looked at, but not by the board: they're the management's job – don't confuse the two!)

Plan the agenda of your board meetings carefully to make room for key matters. Allocate time; I guarantee that if you consider approximately six things you want to achieve this year and make space for them in your board calendar, you will at least address some of them.

## The time and the place

Any board meeting running longer than four hours is unlikely to

[*1] See Structure, section 5, p. 12

be constructive; people will have lost concentration and be delving into too much detail. The chair should manage the time spent on issues as well as the agenda content.

Good days for meetings tend to be mid-week. Try to avoid Mondays and Fridays – particularly when you are using non-executives who may live or work out of the area and be less inclined to travel on these days. Studies have shown that midmorning is when we are most alert and awake, so avoid afternoon slots, particularly after a lunch. It's better to finish with a lunch than start with one.

Keep the room light and airy, switch off mobiles and discourage all unnecessary interruptions. Bring in external stimulation by inviting presentations on particular board issues to encourage creativity and, more importantly, ensure you make decisions. That is your job, after all!

You must keep good-quality minutes. These should record decisions, not discussions, and they should be time-framed with accountability clearly noted. This will help you meet your compliance requirements and provide an excellent template for implementation.

The board meeting should be the heart of the business, so communication after the event should also be considered. How you do this will depend on the size and culture of your business, but I guarantee that failing to communicate at all will simply mean bad governance – and bad governance usually means ultimate failure.

By the way, you may be surprised to know that having your opinion recorded in the minutes is not your legal right, unless you can prove that the decision being made could be a potential source of failure for the company. If you find yourself in a position where, for whatever reason, your point is not being recorded, and if you are uneasy about this, a formal letter to the chair (possibly even copied to the auditors and lawyers) could be of value at a later stage if litigation looms. Such an action isn't necessarily very career-enhancing, but it could ultimately be part of your personal fireguard!

# 3. *Caveat emptor*

There are more fools among buyers than among sellers.
**French proverb**

The principle of *caveat emptor* ('Let the buyer beware') is generally accepted. This means that in most cases, subject to certain
consumer protection principles, the law will not put right a bad
deal. So you paid too much for your new photocopier? Tough.
Being able to take action against the vendor is highly unlikely
unless some sort of fraud is discovered.

However, *caveat venditor* ('Let the seller be on his guard') is of
interest in this context. The principle here is that if the buyer
makes known the purpose of their purchase and the vendor
recommends goods to fulfil that purpose, the vendor is effecting
to guarantee that those goods will be suitable for carrying out
that function. This only applies, however, when the requirements
are expressly communicated, if not then the seller can assume the
goods are for the 'normal purpose' which may of course not be
the same as the purpose actually used.

Contract law is generally complex and all sorts of conditions
apply.

The best advice is openness and clarity in any transactions.
Then both sides can have little recourse to law.

# 4. Financial papers

I do not think much of a man who is not wiser today than
he was yesterday.
**Abraham Lincoln**

Ultimately, whatever the remit of your business, it either needs to
pay its way or have a very benevolent parent indeed hovering in

the background! Financial performance is an incredibly important barometer of success. And as financial papers are the tools
by which you report and communicate its performance to
external and internal parties, they need to be well put together.

The quality and format of these papers, as well as how efficient
you are at making them available, can frankly make the difference
between good and bad performance in a business.

Often you will have covenanted to provide financial information to a funder as part of an investment agreement. But even if
you haven't been, monitoring your performance should be a
regular activity of a good manager.

Availability is one of the first things to consider – when the
information is actually issued. As a minimum, your monthly
accounts pack needs to be issued no later than seven to ten days
after the end of the month. Yes, I know – you won't have received
all the information by then. So you'll need to estimate, as it's
better to have timely information that's 80 per cent accurate than
information that's 85 per cent correct, but received too late to be
remotely useful.

All financial data is subject to error, and management accounts
inevitably include a degree of assumptions, so it will **never** be 100
per cent correct. These are management tools you need then to
manage, and you need them on time.

## On the receiving end

Who should see the information? Subject to the usual confidentiality issues, I suggest as many people as possible. By sharing
information, the responsibility of performing well can be shared
or at least accepted by those people who can make a difference.

And what about discussion dissection and action planning?
While it's true that finances don't tend to be quite as sexy as, say,
marketing and sales, it is fairly critical for there to be a basic level
of understanding. You'll need to get a take on the differing levels
of knowledge and skills within your group to decide which staff
members need training, explanation or both.

One thing that will help everyone grasp what needs to get across is clear, concise presentation. So when putting together a financial pack, the old adage of a picture saying a thousand words works extremely well when you need to explain finance to managers who have little to do with it.

Think pie charts and bar charts to demonstrate variances, market shares and the like. Lots of numbers on loads of pages is not necessarily helpful to anyone other than the detailed analyser. Stick to key performance indicators – and by that I mean, think six or seven items that could 'turn the gas up' on your company if you get them right.

In other words, if you measure these and perform well, then generally the business is going in the right direction. And if you aren't, then it keeps you focused very well on where remedial action needs to be taken.

A written summary of how your business is performing is also very useful, not only to the non-financial manager but also to non-executives and external parties who need to get that 'flavour' of what's going on, which may not always be readily evident from mere numbers and pictures. Keep this summary to bulleted points, and be specific: long, rambling reports are both boring and useless.

## Last touches

Benchmarking and comparisons are very important. You can utilise previous performance or budgeted expectations, or indeed resort to industry comparisons, though be wary of the latter. Don't compare your company to something that actually isn't the same thing: it's like trying to find out why your apple doesn't look like their orange!

Cash is usually critical for business survival and is **not** the same as profit. Make sure you look both at current cash generation and future cash needs as part of your financial reporting pack.

So as a minimum, this pack should contain:

- A balance sheet and profit and loss account compared to budget and prior year

- A rolling cashflow forecast
- A cash statement (how much cash have you created to date)
- A key performance indicator matrix
- A summary written report.

Obviously you may have some specifics related to your industry that you need to measure, and possibly these may be outside your key performance matrix. But watch that the paperwork doesn't become burdensome either in preparation or review. Think clarity and specifics.

# 5. Fraud investigations

> There is no such thing as justice – in or out of court.
> **Clarence Darrow, American defence lawyer**

Nobody wants to believe that fraud could occur in their business. But the fact is that it's much more common than people imagine. A large number of frauds are neither discovered nor reported, and lots of organisations prefer to just deal with such matters internally. The fraud is nearly always committed by a trusted employee who has been given too much power and no appropriate supervision.

Very often, the fraud has been going on for some time, with few obvious signs to allow for discovery.

Certainly, however, there are a few indicators that should cause alarm bells to ring. You have only to remember the Mirror Group and Maxwell to see them – but that's easier in retrospect, and not so obvious at first glance.

What might these be? Here are a handful:
- Key staff who never take holidays
- Staff who always stay late for no apparent reason
- Extravagant lifestyles not in sync with salaries

- Large proforma payments to new suppliers
- No delegation of basic duties
- A high level of security on computers, preventing access by others.

Of course, it's also important not to jump to conclusions. Accusations that are ultimately unfounded could create substantial claims for breaches of human rights as well as basic employment law issues. So it is sensible to take advice, and retain and preserve evidence.

But you need to know how to preserve it. Evidence can soon become corrupted, making it inaccessible. For instance, did you realise that simply turning a computer on or off could cause damage to an essential audit trail? So never touch a computer if you think it may contain essential evidence.

## Just the facts

Do not detain people unless you are pretty certain of the facts, as otherwise you could be accused of false imprisonment (a criminal offence). And of course never, ever physically touch someone, as at the very least this could be deemed common assault.

Be wary also of entrapment. Covert cameras and listening devices are almost always going to be inadmissible as evidence at best and at worst could create a case that favours the defendant.

As usual, prevention is the best form of defence.

Look at your risk management procedures, remove dominant management regimes (where just one person or a few people are in control of data or financial systems), and look at your control procedures.

It has been said that more than 70 per cent of people would commit a crime if they were certain they wouldn't be discovered – a figure that should spur you into action. If your assets don't have adequate protection, get it for them now.

# 6. 'Free' legal help

There's no such thing as a free lunch.
**Anon**

Legal advice is expensive, but there's no way round it – we need it, not just to build better businesses, but also to protect them. We are increasingly litigious as a country and 'trial by tabloid newspaper' doesn't improve matters.

So it's well worth taking advantage of the numerous 'free' legal helplines that are now available. The word 'free' is a little misleading. Very little actually is free as such, but some membership organisations, including the Federation of Small Business (FSB) and the Institute of Directors (IoD), along with many local Chambers of Commerce, offer a 24-hour legal advice line as part of the membership benefits. Advice is available for both businesses and individuals, and in some cases not just 24 hours a day, but 365 days a year. It covers a multitude of areas but can be invaluable when you're tackling employment-related issues, where it is hugely important to take the correct action from the start.

The legal advice would naturally not be the only real benefit of joining one of these organisations or indeed any other that provides this sort of added value, but it certainly does help justify the membership costs. As you'll know, legal advice can soon run into thousands of pounds if not tens of thousands, so taking advantage of free advice early on can set you on the right track and potentially help you save money, even if it eventually becomes obvious that you will need to engage your own personal adviser.

Some organisations will even go one step further and provide an insurance-related facility that basically provides for costs of cases lost to be underwritten, provided that their advice has been taken. This is most often available in the areas of employment tax and health and safety. For small to medium-sized enterprises, which often find it tough keeping up with the compliance requirements all on their own, this kind of option has got to be worth serious consideration.

# 7. Legal professional privilege

A court is a place where what was confused before becomes more unsettled than ever.
**Henry Waldorf Francis, author**

You would only need to watch the occasional television legal drama to gather that what you say to your lawyer is, without your express consent, for their ears only. And on the whole, that's correct. However, there are some important exceptions you should be aware of.

First, this very special privilege of non-disclosure belongs to you as the client. It does not cover correspondence from third parties or information or documents that were not created for the primary purpose of seeking legal advice.

To determine this, you can apply the 'dominant purpose test': if the dominant purpose of the data or communication was not for either litigation or the seeking of general legal advice, then the privilege of non-disclosure does not exist.

Clearly, not having this privilege could cause you all sorts of problems, particularly if you had misguidedly thought that you had it, and had passed information on or created data that was now discloseable or seizable by the relevant authorities. For instance, the Health and Safety Executive, and H M Revenue & Customs could seize information that could then be used against you!

Make sure that any reports you create following a health and safety incident are written with the explicit understanding that they are for legal advice purposes. Otherwise, it's highly possible that the report won't be protected under legal privilege rules and the other side in an action can have full access to its contents.

Take advice as soon as possible about what is privileged and what is not.

# 8. Reasonable v. best endeavour

> All of us, at certain moments of our lives, need to take advice and to receive help from other people.
> **Alexis Carrel, *Reflections on Life***

You'll most likely be familiar with the phrases 'reasonable endeavour' and 'best endeavour' – they're negotiated to death in every manner of commercial agreement.

The lawyers on both sides are, of course, seeking to manage and wherever possible minimise risk for their clients. One often hotly debated clause is the one that relates to completing a particular issue, such as providing all information on time to allow a task to be completed. In this context, reasonable or best endeavour refers to specific actions the company needs to take in completing that task.

But do such clauses really make any difference? The answer is an emphatic YES!

## Best endeavour

A best endeavour clause is much more onerous than one for reasonable endeavour.

Although such a clause is not necessarily as strict as an absolute obligation, in practice what a business that has accepted a best endeavour clause must do is to take action to secure the stated delivery of whatever is required, although the costs and the degree of difficulties that would incur are taken into account. The company would not be expected to take actions that could leave them in financial distress, for instance, but incurring some costs which are reasonable would be expected.

It's important to note that this decision is taken by reference to the facts available at the time of performance, not at the time of contracting! So when the judges or lawyers are arguing whether best or reasonable endeavours are fair in the circumstances, they'll look at the current situation in relation to the contract, not at how the parties saw the issues at the point of signing the contract.

## Reasonable endeavour

A reasonable endeavour clause is much less onerous than one for best endeavour. In fact, it doesn't require the obligator to incur any costs at all.

But clearly, the very best of all would be a specific obligation underwritten by a guarantee, if your company is the one that wants to enforce the requirement; or at the very least, some very specific drafting of the exact obligation.

# 9. Road traffic issues

The government solution to a problem is usually as bad as the problem.
**Milton Friedman, US economist and advocate of Laissez-faire Capitalism**

Have you ever sent your secretary/temp/receptionist out to deliver some post, or deposit something at the bank, or even buy a bottle of milk? This may be deemed to be company business, so are they insured for it?

You need to know that if they're not insured, **your company will be liable** if they have an accident. Needless to say, the consequences of this could be substantial.

Take this scenario. Your secretary drives to the bank to do some business for you. On the way, they knock someone over. Afterwards, the insurance company say that as this was a business trip, your secretary's car insurance isn't valid!

It's not a pretty picture. And this issue also affects people who perhaps work at several depots, or possibly even one of your staff as they attend a training course in another location.

So what are your options? If you have a fleet policy – insurance for a number of vehicles you own – you may be able to get further cover on this for occasional business drivers, such as your secretary. If, however, you have no fleet policy, you do need to ensure that all employees provide you with evidence of their own insurance, and you'll need to police this to ensure compliance. And don't forget any temps!

> One client sent his temp to pick up a manager from the airport. She had a car accident – thankfully not a serious one. But her own insurance was found to be invalid, and the company had to pick up the costs.

To ensure you don't get any nasty shocks in this area – beef up your policies on staffing procedures, sooner rather than later.

# 10. Written v. verbal contracts

> A jury consists of twelve persons chosen to decide who has the better lawyer.
> **Robert Frost**

For a contract to be binding, you need to have several elements in place.

First, there's the 'invitation to treat' – something that invites you to make an offer. An example is a price tag.

The second element is the offer itself. The third element is, of course, acceptance of your offer. Then, what's called consideration must pass between the two parties to the contract. Consideration is some form of value – such as money, although a sum less than value would not in itself make the contract invalid.

For the contract to be binding, it must be for the supply of legal goods and services. So (to take an extreme example) an agreement to supply narcotics to a drug peddler would not be a binding contract, as the product is an illegal one.

Finally, the contractors must have what is called capacity – which is, simply, the ability to enter into a contract. A minor, for instance, will lack capacity and so won't be able to enter into a legally binding contract.

The question is, does a contract need to be in writing to secure its enforcement, assuming all the above criteria are met?

Some contracts are unenforceable unless they are in writing, for instance the sale of a house. However, in most circumstances a verbal contract will be just as binding as a written one. The problem, of course, is one of evidence.

However, anything in writing that's appropriately worded and has all the correct conditions in place will have a much more likely chance of enforcement than one that isn't.

As Sam Goldwyn said, 'A verbal contract isn't worth the paper it is written on.'

# Tax and accounting: number crunching

There's no business like show business, but there are several businesses like accounting.
**David Letterman**

We all know that tax and accounting practices are not particularly thrilling to any but a few professionals. But however dull this area seems, it's still essential. Even the smallest of business owners will periodically need to apply their mind to 'the numbers' at certain points in their organisation's life cycle.

That may not mean an easy ride, however. Tax regulations are a constantly changing minefield filled with statutory amendments and case law interpretations. Bi-annual budgets are only half the story, as the political animal is ever busy driving the fiscal feast. As H M Revenue & Customs is generally a bad loser, it is vital to ensure your tax records are full and accurate, and payments prompt. Avoiding negotiation on an error or omission should be a priority.

## The right adviser

With auditing seen largely as a 'must have' way to compliance for many businesses, the thought might have crossed your mind that going for the cheap and cheerful might be a good move, as long as your business has a sound financial structure. But although such a choice may fill the legal requirement, it is a rare director indeed that cannot buy a better deal from a more appropriate provider.

A good accountant and/or auditor can add real value to your business if you treat them not as a mere provider, but a partner in the business instead. Choosing the right one will repay you immeasurably, not just in terms of the cost of complying with laws and regulations but, more importantly, by pre-empting pitfalls.

As many people 'don't know what they don't know' in relation to tax and accounting practices, securing an appropriate relationship with the right advisers will also ensure you're informed, and in a much better place to make decisions.

# The right information

Finance and numbers rarely seem as sexy as sales and product development. But at the end of the day all directors have a legal requirement to be sufficiently knowledgeable about the finances of their business so they can carry out their duties – quite apart from the commonsense attitude that if you don't create cash you are simply not going to survive.

The use of appropriate reporting tools such as key performance indicators [1] can take most of the pain from this process, as well as making you, as an internal team, more accountable and externally more credible.

Not every business can afford a full-time finance director or an all-singing, all-dancing finance team. And it's true that this is often a luxury that won't bring immediate value. But as your business develops, you'll need to keep your antennae tuned to catch just the right moment for taking on that overhead. Too soon and you'll leave your finance team kicking their heels, while incurring a high overhead; too late, and the business will lack the data that's vital for making informed decisions.

[1] See Tax and accounting, section 9, p. 172

# 1. Audit costs

> It is no use saying, 'We are doing our best.' You have got
> to succeed in doing what is necessary.
> **Sir Winston Churchill**

Audits may seem gruelling, but they are important for showing that your business is reliable. However, as you'll be aware, not all businesses are legally required to have an audit. Recently, the minimum rate of turnover before you need an audit changed from £1 million to £5.6 million.

The role of the auditor is to review the financial information produced by your company and to report to the shareholders whether it represents a true and fair view of the company's performance and state of affairs. Because audited information undoubtedly carries far more weight in terms of its reliability than unaudited information, in terms of a credit rating it is almost certainly going to have far greater recognition than non-audited data.

External shareholders and would-be acquirers or investors are also going to prefer audited accounts, not least because they may then have a route to making a claim if they have relied on the data to make an investment decision.

All this aside, however, there is no reason to pay more than necessary for what may well be a legal necessity.

## Counting the cost

The cost of an audit is no indication of service or value for money. In fact, although the larger auditing and accounting organisations will almost certainly be more expensive than their more modest counterparts, they may be wholly inappropriate for a small or medium-sized business.

What you do need to look for is the quality of advice and the relationship you have with the person or persons giving that advice. In other words, have you got access to the partner running your audit, do you feel comfortable speaking to the team in charge of the process, are you confident in their ability to do a good job for you and your company?

But back to that vexed question: how much to pay. When you consider this, remember that seeing an audit as a necessary evil and keeping costs to a minimum because of this is potentially losing out on an opportunity to improve your corporate performance.

So go for the best auditors you can afford. Don't just stick with mediocrity out of habit. Do you know that people change their spouse more than companies change their auditors, and that part of that is certainly due to complacency?

# Getting the most from auditors

Some recommendations on getting the best from your auditors are as follows.

'Beauty parade' your auditors every three to five years. By that, I mean check they are keeping up to date with technology and your company needs. Ask them to re-quote and benchmark their quote against the competition.

When asking for a quote, here are some top tips:

1. Ask for a fixed price for the audit.

2. Ask for a separate quote for the tax computations, both for the company and for the directors.

3. Ask for an hourly rate for ad hoc advice, and how this is charged – that is, do they charge for telephone support, travelling time and the like?

4. What are their disbursements and mileage policy?

5. What can you do to keep costs down?

6. Ask for at least two interim meetings to be provided for in the fixed quote to allow for tax planning and so on.

7. Ask who will be carrying out the compliance work. (You don't want a partner doing this work at their charge-out rate, and equally you don't want a trainee giving crucial advice.)

8. Ask what they can do for you that other auditing practices can't.

9. Don't forget: every professional practice expects to write some time off on a piece of work so don't be afraid to ask for timesheets if you feel you are being overcharged.

10. Make sure your advisers totally understand your systems and IT. The last thing you want is their learning your system and charging you for the privilege!

# 2. Benefits in kind and dispensations

Benefits in kind – earnings paid in goods rather than cash. Used to be kind to the pocket, but now so only at the margin; thus 'fringe' benefit.

Some say that nobody should keep too much to themselves. The Inland Revenue is of this opinion.
**From the Chartered Institute of Taxation website**

The provision of 'benefits' in addition to a salary is, of course, commonplace, and more often than not attracts both income tax and national insurance charges, the latter affecting both the employer and employee. It therefore makes sense to look at the most effective way of giving and managing these benefits for both parties.

As an employer, you are legally obliged to keep and maintain proper records of all taxable benefits, which are summarised annually on a P11D (it is possible in certain circumstances to get a dispensation not to produce P11Ds). Submitting this government form on time and in an accurate manner is important, as errors attract penalties of up to £3,000.

There are lots of rules and guidelines in relation to benefits, which can be for a whole raft of things including accommodation, interest-free loans, cars and many, many more areas, but basically anyone who earns more than £8,500 per year or is a director is liable to pay tax on the benefits they receive.

The taxable value is a moveable feast that's often amended at Budget time by the Chancellor and linked, in the case of IT equipment for instance, to various initiatives, and in the case of cars to environmental incentives.

It is worth looking very closely at the taxable cost of certain benefits. In some cases this can be reduced effectively by a contribution towards the cost from the employee.

## Non-taxable benefits

Not everything (thankfully) constitutes a taxable benefit, but it is worth asking H M Revenue & Customs for clarification if you are uncertain. However, as a general rule, the following would not be taxed:

1. Employer pension payments into an approved scheme.

2. Subsistence in staff canteens or workplaces.

3. Workplace nursery places.

4. In-house sports facilities.

5. PCs and links to the office from home.

6. Mobile phones and faxes.

7. Relocation expenses up to £8,000.

8. Childcare of £50 per week from April 2005.

9. Education and training.

10. Workplace parking.

11. Approved mileage rates.

12. Professional subscriptions.

13. Personal incidental expenses.

14. Working at home.

15. Eye tests/spectacles.

In relation to taxable benefits, as well as the usual company car and private petrol, loans of over £5,000 given on a beneficial or interest-free basis, private health insurance and home telephones are all taxable if the costs are met by the employer.

So finally you can go out and celebrate. In fact, the HMRC will allow you to provide a social function for staff as a non-taxable benefit provided it is for no more than £150 per head! Yippee!

# 3. Cash accounting

> 783 – the Devil's number (including VAT). Where there's a will there's a tax shelter.
> **From the Chartered Institute of Taxation website**

The threshold for registering for VAT changes periodically with the Budget but is a relatively modest amount, and only the very small business will find it does not pass this critical level fairly quickly.

Being VAT registered has its pros and cons, of course. If you are a business-to-business provider, charging VAT makes little or no difference to your competitive position per se; but if you are selling to the general public, a non-registered business has clearly got the potential to be considerably more cost-effective.

But this may only be part of your problem. If you are over the VAT threshold or have aspirations to be and therefore have registered for VAT, what you will also be aware of is that you may well be in a position of making a payment to Customs & Excise in advance of receiving the payment from your customer – not the best of cash management techniques.

In order to recognise this dilemma Customs & Excise have a scheme called 'cash accounting'. This is applicable to more substantial businesses – currently those with a turnover of less than £600,000 per year, which increases on exit to £750,000 per year (both these figures tend to move at Budgets) – and allows them to pay VAT over to Customs & Excise only when they have actually been paid by their customers. Naturally, their input tax has to be treated in the same way – that is, they only deduct tax on payments made to suppliers.

Clearly this does not suit all businesses. Anyone in retail would get little benefit from such a scheme. There are also exempt businesses, including hire purchase and conditional and credit sales, which will not be able to participate.

However, where you may have to give extended credit to secure a deal (up to a maximum of six months), cash accounting is worthy of serious consideration.

An alternative would be to make a request for payment to a customer rather than issuing a full VAT invoice. The tax point is then delayed until the cash is received, and VAT is only accounted for at that time. Many professional accountancy and legal practices utilise this technique.

# 4. Contingent liabilities

In the business world the rear view mirror is always clearer than the windshield.
**Warren Buffett, wealthy American investor and businessman**

A contingent liability is a potential liability that a company's directors and auditors acknowledge, but think is unlikely to crystallise, or find difficult to quantify.

There are a few interesting points about these liabilities. First of all, they are recorded only in the notes of the accounts – and usually somewhere near the back. (A good technique for analysing accounts, by the way, is to read the notes first, starting at the back of the book and working your way forward!) As there is no liability recorded against the balance sheet, the actual sums involved are neither recorded as reducing profit in the profit and loss account, nor reducing net assets.

So the questions you should be asking when reviewing someone else's information as to their credit-worthiness are:

1.  Is there a good chance of this contingent liability becoming a real liability?

2.  If it does become payable, can the company in question afford it?

If the answer is possibly yes to the first question and probably no to the second, you have a problem – or rather, they do.

A client whose products and services included the provision of warranties for five-year periods post sale had habitually included a contingent liability for the costs of servicing those potential warranty claims in their financial accounts.

Over many years of trading, no claims had ever been received; and when the shareholders received an offer for their company, which they decided to take, they had no problem in providing an indemnity to the new owners that, although the potential for a liability existed against these warranties, they believed it would not crystallise.

Sadly, this wasn't to be the case, and when what turned out to be a batch of faulty goods resulted in a barrage of claims, the vendor in question had rather more to pay out in indemnities than they had ever anticipated.

Of course, you may be in the position of wishing to record your own contingent liability. The final decision as to whether a liability is contingent or not does rest with the directors, though clearly the auditors have to feel comfortable with that decision or your accounts may be qualified (see 'Qualified accounting', starting on page 179).

So remember: peruse your accounts books back to front – and then proceed with caution.

# 5. Depreciation methods and charges

Finance is the art of passing currency from hand to hand until it finally disappears.
**Robert W. Sarnoff, media executive and Chairman of RCA**

If you buy something, such as a car or a piece of furniture, that item in all likelihood will have lost some of its value by the end of a given period. This is known as depreciation – the process by which we recognise the cost of using a fixed asset (such as land, buildings or machinery) in our business. In accountancy terms, depreciation is factored in such a way of providing for a fixed asset's reduction in value.

The amount of depreciation you allocate affects your profitability, although not your taxable profit. That is affected by capital allowances – the write-down allowed by the government – and can be quite different from your depreciation amount.

There are some fairly useful standard percentages linked to depreciation, such as 15 to 20 per cent for fixtures and fittings and plant, 25 per cent for vehicles and $33^1/_3$ per cent for computers. But these are not mandatory, and it is quite feasible for you to choose an entirely different percentage – provided, of course, that your auditor accepts this! And if you select your percentage rate, you can also select your method of depreciation.

## Choosing your method of depreciation

The two methods commonly used are called straight line and reducing balance. You should, of course, use the method that reflects the true value of your assets at any given time.

With straight line, the rationale is that the asset in question has a finite life and that at the end of the write-down period the asset will have either no real value or a known residual value. Such a method is therefore wholly appropriate with, say, IT equipment.

Reducing balance, on the other hand, acknowledges that the said asset has an inherent value and that this will always be so, however much time passes. So this method effectively makes your profit and loss account healthier than straight line depreciation.

Have a look at the table below for a comparison of the two methods.

**Asset value £10,000 at 25% depreciation value**

|  | **Reducing Balance** Company One | | **Straight Line** Company Two | |
|---|---|---|---|---|
|  | Balance Sheet *NAV | Charge to Profit & Loss Account | Balance Sheet *NAV | Charge to Profit & Loss Account |
| Year 1 | 7,500 | 2,500 | 7,500 | 2,500 |
| Year 2 | 5,625 | 1,875 | 5,000 | 2,500 |
| Year 3 | 4,219 | 1,406 | 2,500 | 2,500 |
| Year 4 | 3,165 | 1,054 | - | 2,500 |
|  |  | 6,835 |  | 10,000 |

* Net Asset Value

# 6. Goodwill and brand accounting

A tax inspector is someone who persists in holding his own view even after we've enlightened him with ours.
**From the Chartered Institute of Taxation website**

Real riches are the riches possessed inside.
**B. C. Forbes, financial journalist and *Forbes* business magazine founder**

As the owner of a company, you probably feel your business has a value over and above that of its net assets – value that reflects the essence of your business, whether that is its name, customer database or the quality of its management. And certainly, in the quoted company marketplace, most city analysts would like brand value to be more widely recognised in accounts than they are at the moment.

In private companies, goodwill – that intangible asset that hinges on your company's reputation – is in the eye of the beholder, so to speak. In other words, any enhancement to the value of this asset only really exists if someone else is prepared to pay for it. Both the Companies Act and general financial management principles say that only purchased goodwill should be recognised as an intangible asset.

One particular transaction I recall when there is no doubt that goodwill was being purchased went as follows.

The vendors in this case had had a particularly successful business, long established and historically very profitable, and they had managed to build themselves into a leading brand in their field.

Sadly, and for a variety of reasons, profits began to decline steeply, yet the owners continued to live, with some extravagance, off their business. It began to slip into insolvency, with a balance sheet net worth of less than £1m and little or no tangible assets other than a building.

However, it was still a very well-known brand, which is why my client wished to acquire it, offering them £5.7m for what could, in part, be termed 'fresh air'!

When goodwill is created via an acquisition – that is, when consideration in excess of net worth is purchased – an asset in its own right is created. And naturally, this strengthens the balance sheet of the acquiring company, at least technically.

## The true value of goodwill

The question is, how valid is that value immediately and in the future? Does it go up or down, or even remain static?

In the case of acquiring goodwill, the old accounting principles allowed either for an immediate write-off to profits or a write-off over an agreed period. However, since 1998, FRS10 – the new guideline for goodwill financial management – has made things less clearcut. In theory, as long as the goodwill you have acquired is capable of continued measurement, you can retain it on the balance sheet indefinitely.

But note that the durability of goodwill you've acquired is assessed on several levels including type of business, the state of the industry and so on. If you believe the goodwill is not reducing in value, the Companies Act states that you will need to make a specific disclosure regarding that in your accounts.

It is also possible (though distinctly rarer) to have negative goodwill. This happens when the price paid for the goodwill is less than the value of its net assets. You may have got a rather good bargain, or perhaps there was an acknowledgement of expected future losses because the business, as it stands, will continue to lose money. Either way, FRS10 requires the negative goodwill to be written back to profits over a given agreed period.

## Brands – handle with care

When the intangible asset resides in a definite item such as a brand name, great care needs to be taken. Companies with a specified brand value have often been hit by problems at a later stage; and however attractive the rationale might be, an error could potentially affect both corporate gearing – that is, the relationship between the debt borrowed and equity invested – and even share price.

But as a brand can, in reality, be disposed of outside the business itself, the brand accounting treatment is not governed by the same principles as goodwill. Thus the argument to allow for both periodic reduction (a loss in the brand's value over time due to shifting fashions, for instance) and infinite life (where the chances of a long-established brand losing its status are almost nil) may be easier to sustain. As these matters have a knock-on effect on profits and shareholder value and are technically complex, you will need expert advice on their treatment before progressing.

# 7. Inheritance tax

Will – Strong intention to proceed. Where there's a will, there's a way of reducing death duties.
**A. J. Carroll, *Bluff Your Way in Tax***

There will always be death and taxes; however, death doesn't get worse every year.
**From the Chartered Institute of Taxation website**

It just doesn't seem fair that once you have passed on to your beneficiaries what you have saved or earned and already paid tax on (and that may mean quite a lot), you can't be sure that it won't be taxed again. Unfortunately, the government doesn't quite see it that way.

Inheritance tax applies to the total estate passed – all your assets less your liabilities, including your share of anything that is jointly owned. It also includes assets that may be held in trust for you. If you retain some benefit from, say, gifts you make (for example, if you gift your home but still continue to live in it and maintain it), this will also be classed as part of your estate.

There are, of course, exceptions. For instance, normally no inheritance tax is payable between spouses (unless one does not live in the UK), and there is a threshold under which no tax is paid. From April 2005, this is £275,000 and, although gifts made less than seven years previously are included in the value of an estate, there are specific allowances which can reduce your estate value, including wedding gifts to your children of up to £5,000 each from parents or £2,500 for a grandchild, and maintenance payments for ex-spouses and dependent children made as a gift are also outside the scope of the tax.

You can also gift up to £3,000 per year to anyone, and this can be rolled forward for one year only, if not used from the previous year. These are all moveable amounts, so keep an eye on changes in the Budgets.

In addition gifts made to a charity of any amount are completely free of inheritance tax, as are gifts to established political parties.

## Start planning now

As inheritance tax is levied at a basic flat rate of 40 per cent on anything over the nil rate band, planning early is key. Here are a few tips.

The taxman can only look back seven years, so any gifts made more than seven years before you die are not included in your estate; nor are gifts that are made out of income as opposed to capital, though the taxman will look carefully at all this, as there must be no dilution of your standard of living to subsidise this gift.

So you need to make a will **now**. This will be hugely important in clearly defining the beneficiaries! Also, if you estimate your estate's value, you may well be able to take preventative measures: time can be of the essence in relation to gifts and the setting up of trusts for beneficiaries.

Finally, it is possible to take out insurance for inheritance tax. This is a fairly specialist area but can be hugely comforting when, for instance, the PEP, ISA and TESSA you thought tax-free actually become part of your estate and enlarge your inheritance tax liability.

# 8. Inventory/stock valuations

Chance fights ever on the side of the prudent.
**Euripides**

Are you valuing your stock correctly? Stock is valued at cost, but what is cost and how do you attribute an increase in value to work in progress?

Obviously, how you value your stock will affect your profitability and your net worth (the difference between your total assets and your total liabilities), so this is an important area to look into.

There are several methods of valuing stocks.

The first and traditional method, and the one accepted as valid by H M Revenue & Customs, is the lower of cost and net realisable value. In other words, you value your stock at cost, or what you believe you will sell it at, whichever is the lower. This still begs the question of what the cost actually is.

Average purchase price is one method of looking at the cost. This is highly suitable if your purchase prices vary dramatically because it works by defining the cost price on an average basis over a given period.

The other two common methods are last purchase price and first purchase price. With these, the whole of your stock holding is valued at either the last or first purchase price.

Finally, there's an alternative method, which works by using a standard cost price for a given time frame. This is a good choice when you can't accurately gauge purchase price. However, price fluctuations will only be picked up when these costs are revisited.

## Time for a change?

From H M Revenue & Customs's point of view any change in valuation method needs to be considered for its validity. If the change is made simply to reflect a more accurate value then it will be considered valid. However, if the change creates a tax adjustment, this may be considered a change in basis and therefore could be challenged as invalid.

Any change in method needs to follow generally accepted accounting principles (GAAP) and be seen as realistic compared to real costs.

You should also note that, in any period, if you change the basis of your valuation, you should change both your opening and closing stock values.

Chopping and changing in this area isn't normally recommended. Once you have settled on a method of valuing stock, it is sensible to keep it until circumstances change. Be aware that any change will be noted in the accounting policies of a set of accounts.

# 9. Key performance indicators

If you can count your money, you don't have a billion dollars.
**J. Paul Getty**

Key performance indicators are a way of quantifiably measuring crucial aspects of your company's performance. They can be used as benchmarks that you set and monitor to find out how your business is performing in particular areas, allowing you to pinpoint what you need to improve.

KPIs may be financial or not, but they only have real value when compared to something else, such as prior performance or a budget, and when they are managed as trends rather than considered in isolation.

Quite a few third parties will be looking at your KPIs – banks, shareholders, customers, suppliers and credit agencies. They use the information they glean in this way to make a raft of decisions about your company.

Because of this, it's advisable to know the point of reference these third parties may be coming from. They will all have different criteria for judging your business; banks, for instance, are primarily interested in security and interest cover. With such knowledge you can then ensure that the information you submit to the public domain is given in full knowledge of its impact on the market.

## What to measure, how to compare

As I've said, a KPI in itself has little value unless it is compared to something else or mapped as a trend. I am a great believer in comparing yourself to yourself – for example, asking what have you achieved this year compared to either what you did last year or what you said you would do this year (your budget). And tracking trends in your KPIs is a great idea. Funders love seeing this in graphical form, as it is very easy to read and has instant impact.

As for choosing which aspect of your company's performance to measure, that depends on what you're seeking to achieve. If you're using some KPIs for internal management purposes, you may, for instance, want to set gross profit targets against which your sales team will be measured and given bonuses. And if you use them with an eye to the third parties you deal with, you'll need to know what they're looking for.

Banks, as I've mentioned, will want to know about interest

cover – that is, how much more operating profit you are making compared to the interest you have to pay. Three times the amount of the interest payable is the usual preference. This gives banks a measure of comfort because if your operating profits go down or interest rates go up, you're still making enough profits to pay their interest.

An equity investor, on the other hand, is probably more interested in the return on equity, and will probably be looking for at least 30 per cent.

A supplier may want to monitor your creditor days (how fast you are likely to pay him!), while a customer is probably more interested in your debtor days, which would give an idea of how efficient your credit control department is.

No one of these is, on its own, any more or less important than another. Indeed, it would be more usual for your particular stakeholder to monitor several KPIs.

## Get tracking

Once you have chosen what is important to manage in your company and begun to track your KPIs, you'll swiftly learn to appreciate what a useful tool this is. Tracked KPIs can be used for a whole host of purposes, from creating performance incentives to enabling you and your team to deal directly with problems much more effectively, as it will be quite clear when things are not going as they should.

Good management practice says that ideally you should monitor half a dozen KPIs, choosing them carefully to ensure they're the ones that make a real difference, and set targets to get to a desired level at a given point in time. And when you can see you're not on track, act quickly to rectify the situation.

Don't forget how important cash is. There are very few companies indeed where cash isn't the single most important part of survival. (Here's a little mantra for you: sales are vanity, profit is sanity and cash is absolutely b——y essential!)

A good example of tracking where cash is tied up in your company is to look at your efficiency at debt collection, creditor payment and stock holding.

The formulas are as follows for annual accounts:

| Trade debtors | x 365 | | Stock | x 365 |
|:---|:---|:---|:---|:---|
| Sales | | | Cost of sales | |

| Trade creditors | x 365 |
|:---|:---|
| Cost of sales | |

These formulas will not necessarily give you a scientific absolute, but consistency is what is important here, and the idea of tracking is to give you a best estimate (and to do so in a regular and consistent manner) of where you are as a company.

Think about it like this. Pay your creditors slower than you collect your debtors (within reason of course, and not so you will get a bad credit rating!), and keep optimum stock levels or even consignment stock (if you can persuade a supplier). If you do all this, you will, quite simply, create cash.

Here is a worked example:

| | **Current Year** | **Last Year** |
|:---|:---:|:---:|
| Trade creditors | £400,000 | £350,000 |
| Trade debtors | £700,000 | £600,000 |
| Inventory/Stock | £240,000 | £200,000 |
| Cost of sales | £2,000,000 | £1,600,000 |
| Sales | £3,000,000 | £2,700,000 |

| | **Current Year** | **Last Year** |
|:---|:---:|:---:|

1.

| Trade debtors x 365 | 700,000   x 365 = 85 days | 600,000   x 365 = 81 days |
|:---|:---|:---|
| Sales | 3,000,000 | 2,700,000 |

|  | Current Year | Last Year |
|---|---|---|
| **2.** |  |  |

$\dfrac{\text{Trade creditors} \times 365}{\text{Cost of sales}}$    $\dfrac{400,000 \times 365}{2,000,000} = 73$ days    $\dfrac{350,000}{1,600,000} \times 365 = 80$ days

**3.**

$\dfrac{\text{Inventory} \times 365}{\text{Cost of sales}}$    $\dfrac{240,000}{2,000,000} \times 365 = 44$ days    $\dfrac{200,000}{1,600,000} \times 365 = 46$ days

So! What does this actually mean in this case?

1. You are collecting your debts in slowly and even slower than the previous year.

2. You are paying the creditors quicker than in the previous year.

3. You are holding less stock days than the previous year.

And in theory at least, this is what that means in monitoring terms:

1. You would have £33,000 more cash outstanding than the previous year or, in real terms, £700,000 (trade debtors)/85 days, that is, number of days this represents = £8,235 x 4 (difference in days between last year and current year) = approximately £33,000. (But just imagine: if you brought the number of debtor days down to a more acceptable 60, you would potentially create £200,000 plus of cash!)

2. This company is paying faster than it did in the previous year (and incidentally, faster than it is collecting its debts – which is not good!).

   The cash differential works as follows: £400,000 (trade creditors)/73 days, that is, number of days this represents = £5,479 x 7 (difference in days between this year and last) = £38,000.

3. Stock management on this example has improved from 46 to 44 days but what if you could get that down to, say, 40 – you

would create £22,000 of cash (£240,000 stock/44 days x 4 to bring it to a target of 40 days).

So – as you can see – by tweaking these days you could possibly create a minimum of almost £100,000 working capital. And this is just one example of the beauty of tracking.

Look at your competitors and benchmark performance (taking care that you are comparing like for like, check your credit rating against these important criteria, and take action if it's not where you want to be.

# 10. Negotiation with VAT/PAYE

Deem – Revenue speak for: 'Let's pretend.'

To err is human – and to blame it on the Inland Revenue is even more so.

Q. What is the difference between a terrorist and a tax inspector?
A. You can negotiate with a terrorist.
**From the Chartered Institute of Taxation website**

If you are being investigated by H M Revenue & Customs (HMRC), the new government department that handles both VAT and PAYE, it can be a very daunting experience. And even if you are not being investigated but are simply unable to make the due payments, you may be concerned about any ramifications.

What you've got to remember is that everything is negotiable – and I mean everything.

Investigations can happen to anyone, as a certain number are conducted on a random basis. You should be aware, though, that inconsistencies in returns and whistleblowing account for a good many other investigations. In some cases, HMRC can claim back taxes for as many as 20 years, so clearly there is quite an incentive to pursue you.

The tax payments that are reclaimed aren't necessarily fraud-related. HMRC is also looking for negligence, and indeed it is assumed that an error or omission is at least negligent.

Although it is a fact that HMRC has substantial powers indeed in terms of detention of personnel and searching of premises, they may not even require the customary police warrants. However, a 'dawn raid' is a rare event and an investigation is much more likely to begin with a formal written notice. They do not have to give you any reason for the query, however – and in any case, as we've seen, that can be totally random.

## Playing it safe

Avoiding the investigation in the first place is clearly best, and while there's no way to guarantee this 100 per cent, ensuring you act in the most appropriate manner can only help you. As you can be fined up to £3,000 per year simply for not keeping proper financial records, this is as good a place as any to start.

Also, don't forget to keep good personal financial records as well. If HMRC has good reason, they can look at your own bank accounts; and where you cannot clearly identify a credit, they may be able to claim it as an unrecorded and untaxed bank receipt!

But you also need to manage what you tell HMRC and how you tell them. Take advice early: there are specialist firms available, or your auditors should be able to help. One easy tip is to only answer the questions you are asked – don't volunteer information, as this could create even further investigations. Hold meetings off site if you can, and provide information and records only when you have checked to see whether the inspector has a legal right to that data.

On average, investigation to settlement can take 18 months. However, a 'faster working' scheme has been introduced that aims to cut the time down to about six months, although you do not have to agree to this. You should also take care in deciding whether this is the right option: if you change your mind, you could be seen as being uncooperative.

You should also be aware that government departments routinely exchange information, and that an investigation by one department may easily kickstart another.

Above all, HMRC needs to collect the sums that are due to them, like many organisations they have targets to meet and deadlines to comply with. Therefore, when negotiating, always bear this in mind: if you make full and frank admissions and agree a reasonable payment plan, you are much more likely to avoid litigation.

One famous investigation involved an individual, who shall remain nameless, who settled on a sum in full and final payment with the then Inland Revenue. Unfortunately, he wrote out a cheque on an account not declared to the Revenue throughout the investigation. Needless to say, that individual ended up serving time at her Majesty's pleasure!

# 11. Qualified accounting

Prudence and compromise are necessary means, but every man should have an imprudent end which he will not compromise.
**Charles Horton Cooley,** *Life and the Student*

What if your auditor said they'd decided to qualify your accounts this year. Would you be overjoyed?

Hardly. Although it might sound vaguely positive, if your auditors want to qualify your accounts, it's nearly always a bad thing!

Essentially, qualification is a statement in your auditors' report that either suggests that the information they have been given to produce the accounts is limited in scope, or that you have failed to comply with generally accepted accounting principles (GAAP).

The auditors' role, remember, is to review and analyse the information in your accounts, and present a report to the shareholders saying whether the information provides a true and fair view of the company's performance. But these days, many auditors are extra cautious.

The large number of corporate scandals taking place has made them more wary than ever of putting their name to anything at all that may set off a litigious action. As a result, qualified accounts are becoming a bit thick on the ground. So much so, that it's a good idea to see whether the accounts of any company you want to do business with have been qualified.

Look out for frequent changes of auditors: this could indicate that the company is seeking a more positive opinion from another auditing firm.

## Who gets qualified?

It's important to know how a qualified opinion arises, however, in case your own company ever has to contend with one. There may be a variety of issues involved. It could be down to limited scope, as I've mentioned; or a disagreement with the client over how a particular item is treated from an accountancy point of view.

The qualification comes in three formats, the most detrimental being adverse opinion. The main issue here is that in the auditor's view, some element in the accounts is so material or pervasive that the document is seriously misleading. A good example would be treating a fixed asset such as a piece of equipment as an overhead.

The next qualification is what is called a disclaimer of opinion. This usually happens when it is impossible to gather certain key facts about the company's financial state. For example, if stock with a value critical to net worth was located in an inaccessible area, say a war zone, and so could not be properly assessed, the auditors would be very likely to disclaim their opinion.

Finally, and of less concern, is an 'except for' qualified opinion. This might be given where the auditors are happy with everything in the account except for one particular item, which demands a qualification requiring an adverse opinion or a disclaimer.

All sorts of companies have their accounts qualified, yet they must still be submitted to Companies House. In the past, even the former Inland Revenue's own accounts have been qualified!

# 12. Tax advantages remuneration

> My problem lies in reconciling my gross habits with my net income.
> **Errol Flynn**

> Money frees you from doing things you dislike. Since I dislike doing nearly everything, money is handy.
> **Groucho Marx**

It is without a doubt a fact that no one really **likes** to pay taxes. But given that they're inevitable, we simply need to get on with it.

The good news here is that there are some ways of softening the blow, when it comes. But you'll need to pick and choose.

Among the many tax-saving devices available, some not only cost a substantial sum to set up but may ultimately prove unreliable as subsequent government changes arise. You may, however, like to consider some of the fairly basic and very low-risk options on offer.

Holidays are as good a place as any to start. With a salary sacrifice scheme, you can provide what is effectively a tax-free benefit. Not everyone will want this, but it is worth considering. And what about providing four times life insurance for death in service (the usual amount is two times)? Employee benefit trusts*[1] provide an option to create wealth based on corporate performance. Dividends (obviously only for shareholder employees) also provide a good tax-minimising opportunity and, of course, employer pension contributions.

Look very carefully at company car policies and take advice on the most effective route. Most accounting practices will have a program they can run for you to evaluate whether a company car scheme is a better option than owning your own. In relation to mileage allowances and capital spent, the rules change periodically on this and you should consider a regular review.

*[1] See Exiting, section 2, p. 186

# Exiting:
# getting out gracefully

People of mediocre ability sometimes achieve
outstanding success because they don't know when to
quit. Most men succeed because they are determined to.
**George Allen, US Republican politician**

The dream of retiring wealthy enough to savour the lotus-eating life is one shared by many – but sadly, all too often it remains a dream. Certainly not always through lack of desire or even lack of hard work, but often through lack of planning.

Exiting your business at maximum value requires time and manoeuvres worthy of the armed forces to maximise value and minimise liabilities. If time is a commodity in short supply, it will be even harder for vendors to obtain their desired price. Generally, vendors think their businesses are worth more than they are, and certainly more than an acquirer wants to pay! But there are many tools and techniques available that will allow both sellers and buyers to move the goalposts closer together, and so complete a deal that satisfies all parties.

The value of a private business is hugely debatable, and liabilities at the time of exit can be difficult to define – or rather greater than desirable. However, liabilities can be managed or at least understood with good-quality advice and support from specialists used to working in this field.

Planning your exit properly, with both the right people and in the right timeframe, will open up alternative routes – and alternative routes mean options. Options are essential to maximise value.

## Finding the right mix

The best exit includes a choice of trade buyers, management buy-outs (MBOs) or a mix of management buy-outs and management buy-ins (BIMBOs), and floats. Only the lucky few will have this range of choice, but it's still desirable if you only have a couple of these options. A choice of deal structure and a clear understanding of risk will also help you achieve a more satisfactory outcome.

And, of course, the best exit route specialists clearly signpost events and provide the vendor with support and encouragement through what is almost always a traumatic and stressful time.

Sadly, not all exits complete satisfactorily or even complete at all, and all vendors should have contingency plans to cope with this eventuality. No deal is done until the money is cleared into your bank. **Never** forget that!

# 1. Deferred consideration

Money talks ... but all mine ever says is good-bye.
**Anon**

When you sell your business, you obviously want to do a deal that reflects its maximum value. After all, you've put heart, soul, years of your life and a lot of money into it, and you deserve it. But deals don't always pan out that way.

When you look at the value of your business, I can categorically tell you that more often than not, your perception of that will always be more than that of a potential buyer.

Valuing a private business is a black art. Any amount of complicated formulas will not necessarily allow you to reach a deal. At the end of the day, a private business is only worth what you will sell at and what someone else is prepared to buy for.

However, there are a number of ways to bridge the gaps in real and perceived value. One of these is the use of deferred consideration.

Deferred consideration works on the basis of agreeing a value for the acquisition but not paying it out to the vendor all at once. The deferred element can be provided by the vendor in one of two forms.

One is loan notes. These are redeemed over a given period and may or may not be subject to a premium. The other is an agreement to make a payment to the vendor at some given time if and when a particular event occurs or doesn't, depending on the contract terms. This event could, for example, be the renewal of a contract or the achieving of sales or profit targets.

The issue for the vendor is always one of security. So with loan notes, although they may have a redemption date and be accruing interest, you need to ask what happens if the company can't make the payment or worse, has still gone bust!

The best security comes via a bank guarantee, although this often isn't available in smaller deals, where all security is already used up. An alternative may be a personal guarantee from the directors of the company seeking to buy; but they will be reluctant and you would probably need to resort to litigation to enforce it!

Insuring the loan note would be nice, and a very limited and very expensive market exists for this, but it has to be said that the cost is often prohibitive.

One idea, though not an infallibly workable one, is to have a convertible loan note – an instrument that allows the so-called debt to be converted back into shares if a default occurs. This may not be of much value if the business is collapsing, but it's otherwise worth a thought.

## Contingent deferred consideration

Contingent deferred consideration is potentially even more risky than the non-contingent sort. This is because it's dependent on the occurrence of an event over which you may have little or no control, particularly if your transaction requires you to leave the board, for instance.

Be very wary indeed of deferred contingent consideration related to profit performance covenants. Profit is very malleable, and one person's definition may not be the same as another's. So either be exact in the terms of reference or choose a more easily definable area, such as sales.

However, for all the negatives, deferred consideration can undoubtedly help move the goalposts on value to more acceptable levels. And it is being seen more and more in deals today, so it shouldn't be dismissed. It helps both acquirers and vendors if properly constructed.

# 2. EBTs, EMIs and all employee share plans

Money is like manure. You have to spread it around or it smells.
**J. Paul Getty**

Providing incentives for your employees is a good thing: staff retention generally pays very well when you look at the huge costs of recruitment. And a happy, motivated team is obviously an all-round boon for your business.

Three ways of providing incentives are worth a closer look. With all of them, take specialist advice to maximise tax savings, and take a medium to long-term view of the potential.

# Employee benefit trust

The employee benefit trust or EBT is a mechanism that allows a company to place shares, which will be for the benefit of employees, into a trust. This is then managed by trustees (ideally independent from the company) on behalf of the staff.

An EBT has several advantages, particularly for those looking at succession planning – that is, identifying and training people to replace key staff once they've moved on. Normally, if you give shares as a gift, you will create both an income tax and an NIC charge; but if you gift shares to a discretionary trust, where the beneficiaries are not formally named, the taxes are delayed until, for instance, the company is sold.

As a result, management has a real incentive to remain with the company, as they have the potential to become owners some time in the future at little or no personal cost.

In addition, corporate tax relief will also be available when the benefits pass to the employees in a form subject to income tax and NIC.

Another advantage of EBTs is that they can create an internal market, provided they are set up correctly.

# Enterprise management incentive

The enterprise management incentive (EMI) is an extremely tax-efficient mechanism that allows you to set incentives for management. It is linked to a share option scheme that allows an individual or group of individuals to purchase shares in the company at a given price set in advance. This allows an employee to 'bed and breakfast' (buy and sell their shares on the same day) and take a benefit if and when the share price rises.

There are some general restrictions on EMIs, including a maximum limit on share value of £100,000 and no more than a £3 million value of shares in any scheme. Also, provided the exercise price is set at a market value, there is no tax or NI charge related to the shares when the option is granted or exercised. And if shares are held for two or more years, the maximum rate of taper relief (see 'Taper relief' starting on p. 192) – where the beneficiary may only have a 10 per cent effective tax charge – will apply.

In private companies, market value is set by negotiation with the Shares Valuation Division of H M Revenue & Customs.

There is no minimum period to hold these options, but generally there is often a maximum ten year exercise period. Approval from HMRC is not always mandatory but, as they can inspect the scheme at any time, it is probably worth seeking in the first place.

# All employee share plans

There are many types of all employee share plans or ESPs, derived from case law and statutory ESP provision. With statutory ESPs, which are linked to an approved profit sharing scheme, the employee is not charged income tax on gains made as long as shares are kept in a trust for a minimum of three years.

In case law schemes, the tax liability will occur if the share scheme hasn't been approved by HMRC.

An ESP needs a separate trust involving three entities (individual or corporate). The trust buys shares in the company; it may have taken a bank loan to do this, using the shares as security. The company then gives money to the trust from its own profits, which the trust then uses to pay off the bank loan, which in turn releases the shares held as security so they can be distributed to qualifying employees.

Essentially, then, an ESP is a combination of an EBT and an approved share distribution mechanism which benefits **most** or **all** employees.

The beauty of these schemes is that the incentive allows ownership potential linked to performance in a tax-effective manner, yet without relinquishing control. They can create internal share markets and allow you to sell your shares to your management without the need for them to be personally hugely indebted.

There are other, more complicated vehicles (including shareholder incentive plans) for transferring share benefits without incurring income tax charges. But you'll need specialist advice if you decide to go for them.

The moral? Take care of your employees … and they'll take care of business!

# 3. Purchase of company shares and financial assistance

The trick is to stop thinking of it as 'your' money.
**Tax auditor**

Generally speaking, a company cannot purchase its own shares. However, under Companies Act regulations, provided certain steps are carefully taken, it may be allowed to.

Further, a company cannot give 'financial assistance' in connection with the purchase of its shares. Such assistance usually means the company paying a sum or accepting a liability so that the price payable by the buyer is reduced, or that the company charges its assets to help fund the deal. There are some relaxations of this regulation for private companies to allow for the company to give financial assistance, but again, great care is needed.

These steps or procedures are hugely important, as failing to follow them will result in the security given to the investor by the company being unlawful and therefore unenforceable, or the transaction becoming void. And if you don't comply with the relevant sections you could, as the company director, find yourself in prison.

# Steps for arranging financial assistance

Financial assistance procedures allow you to refinance your company or, for instance, to progress a management buy-out (MBO) by using the company's own assets to secure funds. This will allow you to access cash you could otherwise be unable to utilise. (In other words the company's cash!)

These procedures – which are known as whitewashing – are as follows. It's vital that you follow them in this order.

1. Resignation of existing directors.

2. Consideration of implications of financial assistance.

3. Swearing the statutory declaration supported by a certificate from the company's auditors.

4. Passing of any relevant resolutions.

5. Execution of documents and completion.

There are other matters to consider, as this is a very serious process.

First, do the company's Articles of Association even allow for assistance to be given? If not, you will need to amend them. That requires a special resolution (which 75 per cent plus of the shareholders have to agree!). And if your company was formed before 1981, you may well have to strike out a specific clause that actually prohibits any financial assistance at all from taking place.

If all the shareholders of the company fail to agree unanimously to the special resolution, you will have to wait four weeks before the financial assistance can be given.

You should know that this process has gone horribly wrong in a number of cases, and directors have ended up being disqualified or worse! Take advice from your lawyer and corporate financiers very early on in a transaction. This is a serious, costly process and it needs to be well thought out.

# 4. Swearing statutory declaration to allow financial assistance

It requires wisdom to understand wisdom: the music is nothing if the audience is deaf.
**Walter Lippman, US editor and writer**

A statutory declaration is a requirement for some transactions. This must be given by **all** the directors of the company, and in relation to financial assistance it needs to contain the detail of the assistance being given.

The essence of the declaration is a statement made by the directors that in their opinion the company is solvent at the time the assistance is being given and will remain so for one year. When the declaration is sworn – and it is done so under oath – the company's auditors must attach a report stating that they have verified the company's data and that, in their opinion, the directors' view is not unreasonable.

This auditors' certificate is very important and will only allow financial assistance to be legal if the company has positive net assets and these are not being reduced or, if they are, are at least covered by distributable profits (that is, your reserves account in your balance sheet account).

This view is clearly subjective to some extent. Will your company remain solvent for one year after you have stripped out funds to pay a vendor, say? Are you **quite** sure?

What is important is how seriously you have considered this. If you go about it in a negligent manner, you may well have committed a criminal offence – and that could mean several unhappy years in a prison cell.

# 5. Taper relief

> Some say that nobody should keep too much to
> themselves. The Inland Revenue is of the same opinion.
> **From the Chartered Institute of Taxation website**

Taper relief was introduced into the UK's taxation system in 1998. Its main aim is to reduce the amount of capital gains tax you have to pay when you sell your shares.

To qualify for this kind of relief, you must have owned the shares for a minimum of two years. Provided you fulfil this criterion, you will only pay 10 per cent tax on your capital gain – that is, the difference between the shares' purchase value and your sale value. In order to ensure you only pay 10 per cent, however, there are a few issues you need to be aware of.

One is that this rate only applies to the sale of business assets. Non-business assets do not qualify, so distinguishing between the two is fairly critical. Business assets are essentially those used in the running of the business, such as buildings, machinery, equipment, debtors and cash.

You need to remember, however, that H M Revenue & Customs may view matters differently from you. Are your business assets **solely** for business? For instance, do you sublet any of your premises? Do you have excess cash resources? If so, taper relief could be adjusted accordingly.

So simple tax planning can greatly help ensure maximum relief is gained. My motto is 'Plan your exit from your business as you make your entrance.'

One recent case I dealt with was very unfortunate indeed for the vendor. He sold his business for £750,000, including the £500,000 he had as a cash balance in the business, thinking he would only pay tax on the gain at 10 per cent. H M Revenue & Customs, however, were not of the same opinion. They said a business of that worth didn't need a half million in cash, and the 10 per cent tax was bumped up to an effective rate of 32 per cent! That really spoilt his year, let me tell you.

# 6. Valuing your business

Money was never a big motivation for me, except as a way to keep score. The real excitement is playing the game.
**Donald Trump**

If you would be wealthy, think of saving as well as getting.
**Benjamin Franklin**

No matter how much someone tells you your business is worth, ultimately it's down to what someone else is prepared to pay, and you are prepared to accept. With this in mind, you may well question the validity of even carrying out a valuation exercise unless it is needed for some HMRC or litigious purpose!

Having said that, unless you are simply 'lifestyling' your business – living well out of it but remaining uninterested in its further potential – it is very interesting at least to have some simple tools at hand to check if you are moving in the right direction.

All sorts of factors influence the value of your business. Many will be outside your control, such as the economy, legislation, consumer preference and the like. There's little point in worrying about these. But other factors enhance or depress value, and these do need to be considered.

Few businesses sell overnight, so grooming your company is an intrinsic part of increasing its value. This grooming period could last years, but it's certain to last months at least. Think carefully about who you are selling to, and consider what it is that will make them pay a premium. Is it:

- Management
- Product portfolio
- Customer list
- Supplier terms
- Future business guarantees
- Intellectual property or patents
- Location of trade?

Whichever it is, ensure you maximise its value. The process isn't dissimilar to selling a house. A property tends to sell better with a well-groomed garden and a newly fitted kitchen!

It is entirely probable that the value will vary depending on the buyer, and unless you have a particular reason not to, you will most likely want to choose the more lucrative deal.

Opportunities for disposal include trade buyers, management buy-out teams, BIMBOs (a combination of a management buy-in with a buy-out, where both existing and new managers are on the buying team), floats (although these are fewer in number than ever before) or perhaps even a simple liquidation of assets.

## Price earnings ratio

One standard valuation method is to look at the price earnings ratio (PE Ratio) – the market price of a share divided by its current or estimated future earnings. You can track the PE Ratio for listed companies in the *Financial Times*, then multiply the amount of your own profits by the figure recorded. But this is clearly a flawed method for two crucial reasons. One is that the PE relates to a listed company, which almost certainly will be far more substantial than your own, and secondly – just what profits are you going to use?

To deal with the first point, clearly an unlisted company is unlikely to have the same PE as a private limited company, not least because of the size differential. The business advice and accounting firm BDO Stoy Hayward maintain a check of the average PE Ratio achieved on private company sales in their quarterly publication, the *Private Company Price Index*, available free on their website (go to the BDO Stoy Hayward website at www.bdo.co.uk/bdosh/website/bdouk/websitecontent.nsf/WebSite/National?Open and follow the link.)

If you use the following formula, you will get a discounted PE Ratio that may be more relevant.

$$\frac{\text{PCPI (PE)}}{\text{FTSE all shares (PE)}} \times \text{Industry sector (PE)}$$

Or currently as a 'quick and dirty' guide, just take 40% of the quoted PE.

As for profits, you normalise the pre-tax, pre-interest figure – meaning, you remove non-recurring items such as extraordinary high remuneration figures or one-off costs, and calculate a weighted average over, say, a three-year period.

This is probably a good first-base guess on a possible valuation. Clearly it takes no account of asset value, nor does it take into account any investment appraisal requirement such as payback. And depending on what type of buyer you are seeking to attract, these may be more relevant.

More sophisticated techniques will take into account issues such as the internal rate of return or IRR. The IRR is the price that an institutional investor would expect to pay with reference to refinancing the business; the rate will be relevant to that buyer. This and the use of discounted cash flow models – which effectively take into account the actual perceived value of money in the future – will probably mean you'll need some professional help with the evaluation. And obviously, if your PE value comes out below a net asset value, you will feel less than inclined to accept such a method!

Whatever figure you eventually settle on, always take as much of it in cash as possible. Paper (or shares) may seem to give you a better deal in terms of pounds, but we all know the vagaries of the stockmarket.

My motto is simple – cash is king because you can count it!

# 7. Venture capital returns and exits

Nobody can ever be too rich or too thin.
**Duchess of Windsor**

When a child smiles, he gives pleasure ... so relax. When a businessman smiles, he intends to be pleased ... so don't relax.
**Samuel Goldwyn, major film producer**

You could be forgiven for believing that the UK venture capital industry isn't actually much of an industry any more. The level of investments over the last few years, particularly in small to medium-sized companies, is disappointingly low. Many local offices have closed down completely; yet more are simply managing out their portfolios.

The trouble is that a large proportion of investments fail, and rather spectacularly. The successes can be equally stunning, which is of course one reason why the returns that many traditional venture capitalists are looking for seem unnecessarily high to the entrepreneurs who seek out the investment from the venture capitalists in the first place.

Returns will, to an extent, depend on the type of investment and the length of time the investment is expected to remain in situ. The greatest returns are anticipated when the exit is either to a trade buyer or possibly a float, though the number of floats in recent years has been particularly low. As a general rule, a 30 per cent plus return, year on year, would be a reasonable expectation.

## Anatomy of funding

Generally, venture capitalists are looking to exit after a certain period that is very often linked to the type of fund they are running, for example it may be linked to European funding. This has in its own right a specific period of availability which is variable but unlikely to be for more than five years. Not all investors are the same, of course. It's a good idea to get a clear notion of their expectations from the fund manager.

Funds from a venture capitalist will come in a variety of forms, and could be a combination of a number of products including ordinary and/or preference shares or convertible loans. Traditionally, they will also require some representation on your board – almost always to be paid for by your company. The ability of this person, who is basically a nominee director, is very important: their particular set of skills will inevitably have a good deal of influence on your board.

There is also some fine print to check.

Check out penalty claims for non-compliance, with covenants attached to the funding. One recent transaction I saw included the right of the venture capitalist to flood the board if management accounts weren't delivered at the due deadline! And watch out also for general conditions of death of a shareholder/director. One deal I supervised prohibited the management from leaving their shares to step-children – an almost ludicrous covenant considering the number of second families around these days, but one which this particular venture capitalist was very reluctant to amend.

Don't forget: everything is negotiable to an extent. But the most important element of a venture capital deal is how confident you can be in their ability to understand and support your business and your strategic plans.

# 8. Warranties and indemnities

Promises and pie-crust are made to be broken.
**Jonathan Swift**

When you come to sell your business, part of the forest of paper that will be created will include a series of promises you've made about your company. The extent and substance of these is hugely important because of the possible financial implications, and they'll be occupying the minds of your lawyers for a large part of the transaction.

As arguing over their content will be a time-consuming and painful process, let's take a look at these promises, which are known as warranties and indemnities.

Basically, a warranty creates a legally binding assurance that relates to an event in the past. For instance, you may 'warrant' that you have never had a negative VAT investigation. If this later proves to be untrue, then – as you have given a legally binding promise it isn't – an action for any damages resulting from that 'lie' can be brought against you.

An indemnity is a legally binding protection against the liability for future events – usually negative ones. It creates a binding obligation on one party to reimburse another for losses that may occur in the future.

## The disclosure process

In a transaction, vendors are naturally very keen to retain all the funds they receive for the sale of the business. They don't want them chipped away by claims from the acquiring company at some later stage. To ensure this outcome as far as possible, it is fairly vital that the vendors leave nothing outstanding that could, at a later stage, result in a claim from the acquirers.

Part of the process of selling your business involves making various statements about its health, wealth, future and history. These could in part, be called disclosures.

Disclosures have become part of the legal documents that form sale and purchase agreements, and are important evidence in the case of action over damages. So they need to be very specific. Of course, no one can recall every little detail about their business, but acquirers understandably want as much assurance as possible before they make the acquisition, so you will need to think long and hard about your own disclosures if you are the vendor. And if the tables are turned and you're the acquirer, you'll obviously want to be happy with the vendor's!

As claims can be made against your warranties and indemnities, you'll need to highlight any links between them and relevant disclosures in the document. For instance, you may want to say that you are 'not aware of any potential employee litigation outstanding [a warranty] except for Mr X's actions for unfair dismissal [a disclosure]'.

In other words, no claim can be made against you in relation to the X case – but if something else occurs that's reasonable for you to have known about, you may have a warranty case.

In managing the extent of these liabilities, a good lawyer will ensure there are both minimum and maximum levels. Minimum being such that irrelevant and time-wasting claims can not be made; and maximum, so as not at the very least to leave you, the vendor, with a liability that exceeds the value of the consideration you received in the transaction.

With indemnity issues, you may sometimes be asked to leave funds for an agreed period in an escrow account. This account, which is usually managed by both solicitors, will be held open until the period agreed comes to an end or a claim is made.

It is possible to get indemnity and warranty insurance. Specialist firms can provide this, obviously at a cost. *De minimis* values – stipulated minimum values that are not payable until the claim reaches a particular level – need carefully vetting, but insurance is certainly worth considering.

# Ever wondered what you didn't know you didn't know?

How savvy a businessperson are you?

Are you a dab hand at directing? Do you know all there is to know about intellectual property, employee rights and tax?

You may feel you'd pass any general knowledge test about running a company with flying colours. Want to try?

Complete this little quiz to test your knowledge. If you score 30 or above, don't worry too much: you probably know enough to get by! Much less, and you may need to worry – or simply be sensible, and dive back into the relevant sections of this book.

## Who wants to be a director?

So you've got a new job title. But do you understand your role and its implications?

**1. What is an executive director?**

a. Someone who is subordinate to the chairman.

b. Someone appointed for his functional expertise.

c. One among equals in the boardroom.

d. Someone heading up a functional responsibility.

**2. From where does a director's authority come?**

a. From the collective decisions of the board.

b. From the size of his shareholding.

c. From the amount of responsibility delegated to him by the chairman.

d. From his executive title within the company.

**3. Just how much should a director participate in board matters?**

a. Only when asked to do so by the chairman.

b. On matters related to his executive responsibilities.

c. Not be critical of executive management.

d. Be prepared to offer opinions or advice on all items appearing on the agenda.

**4. When is an executive director responsible for board decisions made when he's not there?**

a. He isn't if his objection is minuted.

b. On all occasions as a result of a properly constituted board meeting.

c. If the meeting was called without reasonable notice.

d. He would never be held responsible for decisions made in his absence.

**5. When is a director free of his responsibilities to a company?**

a. After he has tendered his resignation.

b. After the company has gone into liquidation.

c. After an administrative receiver has been appointed.

d. Three years after resigning from the board of a company still trading.

**6. Who is responsible for the day-to-day running of a company?**

a. The company secretary.

b. Heads of management departments.

c. The managing director.

d. The chairman.

**7. Who is responsible for filing the statutory returns?**

a. The company secretary.

b. The company secretary together with the board.

c. The board of directors.

d. The auditors together with the company secretary.

**8. Who is responsible for the final wording of the board minutes?**

a. The chairman.

b. The board of directors.

c. The company secretary.

d. The company lawyer.

**9. How much notice does a formal board meeting require?**

a. None.

b. Seven days in writing.

c. Must be announced at the previous meeting.

d. Reasonable time given the circumstances.

**10. When does an executive director have to account to the board for his department?**

a. At every board meeting.

b. When required through the managing director suitably briefed before the meeting.

c. Directly through his department report.

d. Not at all.

**11. Who takes responsibility for setting long-term corporate strategy?**

a. The executive directors.

b. The executive directors plus senior managers.

c. The chairman, managing director and non-executive directors.

d. The board of directors.

**12. Who is responsible for the chairman's decisions?**

a. The chairman.

b. The company and the board.

c. The board of directors, the chairman and the company.

d. The decision is null and void.

**13. Who decides on the constitution of the board generally? Under Table A, Memorandum and Articles.**

a. The board as a whole.

b. The shareholders.

c. It depends on your Memorandum and Articles of Association.

d. The executive directors.

**14. How often legally must a board meet?**

a. Each month.

b. Whenever the chairman decides to do so.

c. As stated in the Memorandum of Association.

d. Once a year to prepare the directors' report.

**15. In a set of accounts what is the director's report for?**

a. To give a forecast of future profitability.

b. To outline market potential in the immediate future.

c. To give an account of the development of the company during the financial year.

d. To announce the dividend which will be paid.

**16. When is it considered reasonable for a director to miss a board meeting?**

a. When he is sick or overseas on business.

b. When he takes his annual holiday.

c. When an important business deal comes up.

d. When it is socially inconvenient to be present.

**17. If you are a lone dissenter in a decision, are you still responsible?**

a. Yes, under collective responsibility.

b. No, you made your position clear.

c. No, this would be against natural justice.

d. Probably not if I threatened resignation.


**18. When should a director insist on minuting his dissent?**

a. On every disagreement of policy.

b. On matters of principle.

c. Whenever he feels he is in the right.

d. When he is a director of a public company.


**19. When has a director the right to have his opinion minuted?**

a. When the decisions made are likely to have a direct bearing on the success or failure of the company.

b. At any time.

c. At the discretion of the company secretary.

d. When the chairman feels that it is justified.


**20. If a company commits a civil offence who would be likely to be considered responsible?**

a. The employee.

b. The board of directors.

c. The employee's manager.

d. The company and its board or a particular director.


**21. In a case of suspected insolvency, who is responsible for taking initial action?**

a. The board of directors.

b. The finance director.

c. An auditors' employee of partner status.

d. The chairman of a creditors' meeting.

**22. To avoid a charge of wrongful trading, whose interests must first be considered?**

a. The company's shareholders.

b. The company's bank.

c. The directors' service agreement.

d. The company's creditors.

**23. Who is responsible if financial accounts are not filed at Companies House on time?**

a. The officers of the company.

b. The company secretary.

c. The board of directors.

d. The chairman and company secretary.

**24. What is the maximum period the courts can disqualify a director?**

a. For 15 years.

b. For five years.

c. For life, if managing director or finance director.

d. None, if the individual is a non-executive director.

**25. What % of votes do you need for a special resolution?**

a. 51%.

b. 75%.

c. 90%.

d. 100%.

**26. Which of these is a civil offence?**

a. Fraud.

b. Trespass.

c. Acting as a director when disqualified.

d. Insider dealing.

**27.** Directors are not allowed to participate in substantial property transactions without shareholder approval. Which of these is a substantial property transaction?

a. 10% of the asset value of a company.
b. 20% of the asset value of a company.
c. 25% of the asset value of a company.
d. 50% of the asset value of a company.

**28.** Directors cannot borrow money from their company except to limited amounts. How much is the amount?

a. Up to £2,000.
b. Up to £5,000.
c. Up to £10,000.
d. Up to £20,000.

**29.** How long can a director's service contract be for before it needs shareholder approval?

a. 5 years
b. 4 years +
c. 3 years +
d. 2 years +

**30.** Corporate manslaughter charges are more likely to be brought against small companies because:

a. You have to prove negligence was committed by the controlling mind.
b. They are less likely to have adhered to the common law code.
c. Shareholders and directors are likely to be one and the same.
d. Corporate manslaughter can only be brought against a close company.

**31.** Under the new offence of corporate killing can individual directors be made liable?

a. Yes.
b. No.

**32. If you act as a director while disqualified, who is liable for the company debts?**

a. The company.

b. The shareholders.

c. You.

d. The board.

**33. When would 'garden leave' be acceptable in an employment contract?**

a. Where the contract of employment provides for it.

b. Where there are sensitive business issues involved.

c. In disciplinary cases.

d. When it is part of a redundancy agreement.

**34. When would a compromise agreement not be binding?**

a. Where a court deems it to be unfair.

b. Where the employee is under 18.

c. Where the employee has not taken independent advice.

d. Where duress has been used.

**35. What is a Romalpa clause?**

a. Restraint of trade.

b. Retention of title.

c. Exclusivity.

d. Disclaimer.

**36. Which organisation deals with issues of product safety? a.**

a. Department of Trade and Industry.

b. Trading Standards.

c. Health & Safety Executive.

d. IIP.

### 37. What is the tort of passing off?

a. To sell goods to which you have no good title.

b. To make your goods appear to have someone else's brand.

c. Copywriting goods that are not original.

### 38. How do you protect your right to a trademark?

a. Register it.

b. Patent it.

c. Copyright it.

### 39. How many directors are required for a quorum?

a. One.

b. Two.

c. Depends on your Memorandum of Association.

d. Depends on your Articles of Association.

## ANSWERS TO THE QUIZ

| | | | | | |
|---|---|---|---|---|---|
| 1 – (c) | 2 – (a) | 3 – (d) | 4 – (b) | 5 – (d) | 6 – (c) |
| 7 – (b) | 8 – (b) | 9 – (d) | 10 – (b) | 11 – (d) | 12 – (c) |
| 13 – (b) | 14 – (d) | 15 – (c) | 16 – (a) | 17 – (a) | 18 – (a) |
| 19 – (a) | 20 – (d) | 21 – (a) | 22 – (d) | 23 – (c) | 24 – (a) |
| 25 – (b) | 26 – (b) | 27 – (a) | 28 – (b) | 29 – (a) | 30 – (a) |
| 31 – (a) | 32 – (c) | 33 – (a) | 34 – (c) | 35 – (b) | 36 – (b) |
| 37 – (b) | 38 – (a) | 39 – (d) | | | |

**If you got:**

**over 32** You are either a lawyer, an accountant or a very highly experienced director. There is no pulling the wool over your eyes: you know exactly where you are and what your responsibilities are in relation to your job role.

**25 – 32:**   I have some concern about your ability, but generally you know enough to get by. It may be an idea to let your fellow directors undertake the same test. Hopefully, if there is an overall understanding, there is no reason why you shouldn't get along just fine.

**20 – 25:**   There are severe holes in your knowledge as to the role and responsibility of the director. If you are already in a post, you need to ensure that you are made much more fully aware of exactly what a director is responsible for. These questions are only a selection of many and there are several other issues that you should understand fully. It is possible that you are already in breach of many of the regulations and are putting yourself at serious personal, financial and professional risk. Take advice quickly.

**Less than 20:** Let's hope that you are not a director. If you are, you definitely shouldn't be. You have taken up a post that incurs both professional and personal liability without any understanding of what these are. If you are not in this role and aspire to be I suggest you do some serious reading. This job is much, much more than a title and a flashy car.

# Glossary of terms

**Accrual** An outstanding expense at the end of a trading period.

**Acid test** A ratio that determines a company's ability to pay its short-term debts – that is, current assets or stock/current liabilities (also known as liquid assets). An acceptable ratio would be 2:1.

**Annual general meeting** A company must hold a meeting of its shareholders each year to deal with various compliance matters, including the adoption of the period year's financial statements, rotation of directors and the appointment of auditors.

**Arbitration** Used to settle a dispute, this is an alternative to litigation whereby the decision is binding on both parties.

**Articles of Association** Part of the constitutional document of the company, the Articles of Association cover the internal regulations of the company, including procedure, shares, meetings, directors and so forth.

**Asset** An item owned by or owed to the business which it needs to help carry out its activities. Assets can either be fixed or current.

Fixed tangible assets include buildings, cars, IT equipment and so on – touchable objects, in essence. Fixed intangible assets include patents, goodwill, brands and the like – items that have a value but that are 'invisible'.

Current assets are assets that are variable in value on an ongoing basis. They can include debtors, cash, stock and so on, which are often called liquid assets because they can be realised quickly.

**Audit** A legal requirement of companies who meet particular financial criteria which allows for an independent party to declare if all financial statements show a 'true and fair view' of the company's state of affairs.

**Authorised share capital** Shares in the authorised share capital are available to be issued. Not all of the authorised share capital needs to be issued but when it is, the person subscribing must pay cash or equivalent value of at least the nominal amount.

**Balance sheet** A statement of a firm's assets and liabilities at a given point in time.

**Bankruptcy** An order made against an individual which states he is unable to pay his debts and provides for his property to be distributed to his creditors.

**Breach of contract** If an agreement that is contractual is broken, the court will seek to ensure both parties are put in the position they would have been in if the breach had not occurred. This is done by the award of damages.

**Break even** When a business earns neither a profit nor a loss.

**Budget** A planned activity/resource or cost for a whole business or department that may incorporate a series of financial papers including, but not exclusively, a balance sheet, cash flow and profit and loss account.

**Business angel** Wealthy individual investors who are looking to invest smaller amounts of capital in companies.

**Capital allowances** Variable allowances set by H M Revenue & Customs periodically for taxation purposes, to cover depreciation in the value of a company's assets.

**Capital gains tax** A tax on the gain made from the sale of an asset.

**Cashflow statement** This shows the movement and availability of cash within a company over a given period.

**Certificate of incorporation** This is the legal document which allows the incorporation of a company to be entered on the register at Companies House and thereby come into existence as a separate legal person.

**Chairman** Usually appointed by the directors and often non-executive, he or she often chairs the meeting as well as the board. He or she may have a casting vote.

**Company** A distinct legal entity governed by company law and separate from its shareholders and directors.

**Corporation tax** A tax charged by the government on company profits, usually paid nine months after the end of the company's accounting year.

**Creditors** Individuals or companies who are owed money for goods.

**Current assets** Anything that is expected to be converted into cash within 12 months of the balance sheet date.

**Current ratio** The relationship between current assets and current liabilities, describing the liquidity of the business. A 2:1 ratio for current assets/current liabilities is credible.

**Current liabilities** Funds owed by the business within the next 12 months.

**Deadlock** Where shareholders cannot reach agreement because the voting on an issue is split 50/50.

**Debenture** Legal document or charge which creates a right, likely to be a financial one, owed by the company to the holder of the charge.

**Debtors** Monies owed by third parties to an organisation for materials or services, which have not yet been paid.

**Depreciation** The apportionment of a cost of a capital item over an agreed period based on its life expectancy. This reduces the value of the assets and the company's profit over the agreed period; it does not affect cash or taxable profit.

**Directors' register** A statutory requirement which lists the details of the business directors and secretary including name, address, occupation, nationality, date of birth and other director-ships.

**Discrimination** The law generally prohibits discrimination against various sectors of the workforce. This occurs if you behave in a manner that may be considered to disadvantage a person from pre-recruitment to termination of a job role.

**Dividend** The distribution of after-tax profits to the shareholders as a reward for investment.

**Due diligence** An investigation into a company to review its value and to run sensitivities on various commercial, financial and environmental points.

**EBT** *et al.* EBT = Earnings Before Tax; EBIT = Earnings Before Interest and Tax; EBIAT = Earnings Before Interest after Tax; EBITD = Earnings Before Interest, Tax and Depreciation; and EBITDA = Earnings Before Interest, Tax, Depreciation and Amortisation, all where earnings = operating and non-operating profits.

**Employee share ownership** A scheme that is approved by H M Revenue & Customs, where employees acquire shares in the company.

**Equity** The amount of share ownership an individual or group has in a business.

**Extraordinary general meeting** Any meeting of the shareholders that is not the annual general meeting is known as an extraordinary general meeting.

**Factoring** The specialist provision by one firm to another by buying its unpaid invoices. The factor will usually provide immediate cash up to the value of 85 per cent or more of the client's invoices, which accelerates the availability of working capital.

**Fixed costs** Those costs that do not vary according to level of production, such as rent or utilities.

**Floating charge** A form of security documentation that creates a charge over a particular asset for security for borrowings and so on.

**Flotation** A company is 'floated' when shares in it are issued to the general public. The company will issue a prospectus inviting shareholders to subscribe for shares at a given opportunity.

**Gearing** The relationship between debt and equity – usually the relationship between long-term borrowings and shareholders' funds. Anything over 50 per cent is considered highly geared.

**Goodwill** Any excess money paid to acquire a company that exceeds its net tangible assets value.

**Gross margin** The difference between the selling price of a product and its cost.

**Implied terms** When goods or services are sold there are certain terms implied. For goods these are satisfactory quality, fitness for purpose, conformity with sample or description and the right to sell the goods. Some implied terms can be excluded or restricted except where the law prohibits it.

**Indemnity** An agreement by a company to compensate a customer for any losses.

**Industrial tribunal** This usually consists of three people – a lawyer (the chairman), one individual nominated by an employer association and another by the employee body. Most cases must be brought within three months of the event.

**Initial public offering** The first sale of privately owned shares in a company via the issue of shares to the public and other investing institutions.

**Insolvency** When a company's liabilities to creditors exceed assets.

**Intellectual property** The value held in copyright, patents, designs and so forth.

**Interim report** Reports prepared half-yearly or otherwise to inform shareholders of the firm's performance.

**Issue price** The price at which a share is issued.

**Job costing** An accounting method that seeks to determine the overall cost of a job by evaluating the time and materials required.

**Licence** An agreement that allows the licensee to do an act which would otherwise be the exclusive right of the licensor. It may be exclusive or non-exclusive.

**Limited company** A company owned by one or more people who contribute funds in return for shares in the company.

**Liquidation** When a company ceases to exist as a legal entity.

**Loan guarantee scheme** A government-sponsored scheme aimed at encouraging commercial banks to provide loan finance to high-risk small businesses whereby the government secures the loan in the absence of corporate and personal security being available.

**Management buy-in** This is when a group of entrepreneurs organise a take-over of a company and form a new management team to acquire an existing business.

**Management buy-out** This is when the existing management team organises a purchase of a firm from the shareholders of a company.

**Memorandum of Association** A constitutional document of a company containing such things as its name, its objects and powers and its original share capital details.

**Minority shareholder** A shareholder holding less than 50 per cent of the voting rights.

**Minutes** A written summary of the proceedings of directors' or shareholders' meetings. Usually prepared by the secretary and approved at the next meeting and signed by the chairman or managing director in his absence.

**Net assets** The sum of a company's fixed and current assets less its liabilities.

**Net book value** The value reflected in the company's books of the worth of an asset, basically purchase price less depreciation to date.

**Net profit** Sales or turnover less overheads.

**Operating profit** Sales or turnover less overheads but excluding interest, tax and dividends.

**Ordinary resolution** A resolution passed by a simple majority – that is, 51 per cent of shareholders at a general meeting.

**Ordinary shares** A share attracting a dividend if available after payment of any preferential dividend, pro rata to the percentage shareholding in the company.

**Paid-up capital** This is the amount of capital paid by shareholders to date.

**Partnership** Two or more individuals who run a business and whose liability for debts incurred is personal and unlimited.

**PE Ratio** Price per earnings or PE Ratio is an indicator as to how the market views performance prospects and risk of a company, reached by dividing the share price by the earnings per share (profit after tax and interest divided by the number of ordinary shares in issue). As earnings per share are a yearly total, the PE Ratio is also an expression of how many years it will take for earnings to cover the share.

To calculate a PE:

Take total profit after tax and interest for the past year, divide this by the number of shares issued; this gives you earnings per share. Then divide the price of the share by the earnings per share; this gives the price/earnings or PE Ratio.

**PLC (public limited company)** Under UK law there is a minimum number of shareholders but no maximum. Shares are bought and sold on the stockmarket by the general public, and the performance and rewards of the company create a market value.

**Pre-emption rights** Where new shares are to be issued, existing shareholders may have the right to be offered a pro-rata part of the new shares before they are offered to a new shareholder. These rights are either in the Articles of Association or imposed by the Companies Act 1985. They can, however, by a special resolution, be dispensed with. These rights also can be made applicable in the sale of existing shares.

**Profit and loss account** An accounting statement for a given period detailing sales and expenses. These are broken into subheadings containing gross profit, operating costs and profits, interest and net profit.

**Proforma** Invoices issued in advance of the shipment of goods or services which are due for payment prior to supply.

**Proxy** A person appointed by a shareholder or director to vote and speak for him at a meeting.

**Quorum** The number of shareholders or directors who must be present at a meeting to allow proceedings to be validly conducted. The default for director quorums is two, though this can be varied by the Articles of Association.

**Receiver** An individual appointed by a funder with a charge over the company's assets who makes this appointment due to payment covenants being breached.

**Redemption of shares** A company can redeem shares by repaying the nominal value to the shareholder. The shares are then cancelled. There must be sufficient reserves to allow this and the share must be of a redeemable nature.

**Register of members** A register must be kept which shows the name and address of the shareholder, the number of shares held, the amount paid up, the number of relevant transfers and any transfers or acquisition of shares.

**Reserves** Those undistributed profits belonging to the shareholder retained in the business.

**Service contract** A legal agreement between a company and its directors or senior managers, setting out their terms of service. It tends to be more detailed than an employment contract.

**Shell company** A company that is listed on the stockmarket but that does not trade and is available to move companies into, to allow for access to the public market.

**Table A** A standard set of Articles of Association as detailed in the Companies Act, usually used to cover non-essential procedural issues. Table A applies to private companies limited by shares. Tables B–F apply to other types of company such as companies limited by guarantee.

**Winding up** Basically, this means settling accounts as part of the liquidation process. Under the Insolvency Act there are three procedures – a member's voluntary winding up, a creditor's voluntary winding up and a compulsory winding up by the court. The administration of the process is conducted by a liquidator who at the end of it will distribute any reserves to shareholders and creditors.

**Yield** The income paid out on an investment, expressed as a percentage of its capital value.

# Recommended reading

Bough, J., *Financial and Accounting Responsibilities of Directors*, Certified Accountant Publications, 1985

Cadbury, A., *New Company Chairman*, Director Books, 1995

*Directors Remuneration: A Practical Guide to Setting the Pay and Benefits of Senior Executives*, Director Publications, 2002

Dunne, P., *Running Board Meetings: Tips and Techniques for Getting the Best from Them*, Kogan Page, 2005

Ginman, P., *The Guide to Directors' Duties and Responsibilities: Your Questions Answered*, Kogan Page, 1992

Hadden, T., *The Control of Corporate Groups*, University of London Institute of Advanced Legal Studies, 1983

Harper, J., *Chairing the Board: A Practical Guide to Activities and Responsibilities*, Kogan Page, 2005

Hemmings, R., *Employment Acts Explained*, The Stationery Office Books, 1999

Institute of Directors, *The Company Director's Guide*, Kogan Page, 2001

Kendall, N., *Good Corporate Governance*, Accountancy Books, 1994

Loose, P. and Read, A., *The Company Director: Powers and Duties*, Jordans, 2000

McNeill, P. and Howarth S., *Company Penalties*, Financial Times/Prentice Hall, 1993

*New Work Habits for a Radically Changing World*, Price Pritchett, 1996

Pierce, C. (ed), *The Effective Director*, Kogan Page, 2001

Souster, P., *Directors' Responsibilities and Liabilities*, Chartac Books, 1990

*Standards for the Board*, Kogan Page, 2003

Tricker, R., *Corporate Governance*, Dartmouth, 2000

Whitaker, J. and Roney, A., *Directors' Duties and Responsibilities in the European Community*, Kogan Page, 1992

Wright, D. and Creighton, B., *Butterworths Rights and Duties of Directors*, Butterworths Law, 1998

# Useful organisations

**The Academy for Chief Executives**
www.chiefexecutive.com
The Nexus Building, Letchworth Garden City, Hertfordshire
SG6 3TA
0800 0370 250
ACE provides a confidential learning environment for non-competing chief executives and managing directors from all sectors of industry, commerce and the non-profit sector.

**ACAS**
www.acas.org.uk
Head office: Brandon House, 180 Borough High Street, London
SE1 1LW
020 7210 3613
ACAS aims to improve organisations and working life through better employment relations. It provides up-to-date information, independent advice, high-quality training and works with employers and employees to solve problems and improve performance.
ACAS has a number of regional offices. Note that you must make an appointment before visiting.

**Association of Chartered Certified Accountants**
www.accaglobal.com
64 Finnieston Square, Glasgow G3 8DT
0141 582 2000
The Association of Chartered Certified Accounting is the largest international accountancy body in the world. Their mission is to provide professional opportunities and access for people of

ability around the world, to achieve and promote the highest professional, ethical and governance standards, to advance public interest and to be the global leader in the profession.

## Companies House

www.companieshouse.gov.uk
Main office: Crown Way, Maindy, Cardiff CF14 3UZ
Contact Centre: 0870 3333 636
The main functions of Companies House include incorporating and dissolving limited companies, examining and storing company information and making all this information available to the public. The site also gives a lot of useful information with regards to running a company.

## Confederation of British Industry (CBI)

www.cbi.org.uk
The CBI's mission is to help create and sustain the conditions in which businesses in the United Kingdom can compete and prosper for the benefit of all.

It is the premier lobbying organisation for UK business on national and international issues. The CBI works with the UK government, international legislators and policy-makers to help UK businesses compete effectively.

CBI policy is decided by its members – senior professionals from all sectors and sizes of business are directly involved in the policy-making process. Its network of offices around the UK, in Brussels and Washington provides on-the-ground support for its members.

## Department of Trade and Industry (DTI)

www.dti.gov.uk
Department of Trade and Industry Response Centre, 1 Victoria Street, London SW1H 0ET
020 7215 5000
The DTI drives their ambition of 'prosperity for all' by working to create the best environment for business success in the UK. It

helps people and companies become more productive by promoting enterprise, innovation and creativity.

It champions UK business at home and abroad and invests heavily in world-class science and technology. The DTI protects the rights of working people and consumers and stands up for fair and open markets in the UK, Europe and the world.

At www.dti.gov.uk/cld/condocs.htm you will find consultation documents on Corporate Law and Governance which include:

Current Consultations

Consultations under archive awaiting a response from the government

Consultations under archive where a response from government has been published

Other relevant Consultations

### Directgov

www.direct.gov.uk

Directgov is the place to turn to for the widest range of government information and services.

Browse by audience groups such as 'disabled people' and 'parents' or by topics including 'employment', 'learning' and 'motoring'. Alternatively, you can access definitive government directories or use the search engine.

As well as government departments, the site links through to relevant third parties which can offer additional trusted advice and support.

### Dun & Bradstreet

www.dnb.com

D&B United Kingdom Customer Service Department, Westminster House, Portland Street, Manchester M1 3HU

0870 243 2344

Dun & Bradstreet is a provider of global business information, tools and insight, enabling customers to make critical business decisions.

**Experian**
www.experian.com
UK headquarters: Talbot House, Talbot Street, Nottingham N80 1TH
115 941 0888
Experian helps organisations find the best prospects and make informal decisions to personalise and develop customer relationships. They support the direct marketing, business information, decision support and outsourcing requirements of over 40,000 organisations.

**Institute of Chartered Secretaries and Administrators (ICSA)**
www.icsa.org.uk
16 Park Crescent, London W1B 1AH
020 7580 4741
With over 100 years' experience, the Institute of Chartered Secretaries and Administrators (ICSA) is the recognised global voice on governance and regulatory issues in the private, public and not-for-profit sectors. Working with governmental and other statutory bodies, ICSA promotes best practice and provides guidance on good governance. As the qualifying body for company secretaries and senior administrators, ICSA offers a professional qualification covering business, company law, corporate governance, management, finance/accounting, administration and company secretarial practice. No other professional body in the business area offers the breadth of knowledge which the ICSA Qualifying Scheme provides.

**The Institute of Directors (IoD)**
www.iod.com
116 Pall Mall, London SW1Y 5ED
020 7839 1233
With a worldwide membership, the IoD provides a professional network that reaches into every corner of the business community. Membership spans a whole spectrum of business leadership, from the largest public companies to the smallest private firms.

The IoD represents its members' concerns to the government and provides professional business support wherever needed. Members receive benefits including advice, training, conference and publications.

Some of the IoD's services are offered exclusively to IoD members and others are available to all users of iod.com. You can access a range of specially selected fact sheets, publications at a discount, services and much more, by the key subjects listed below at www.iod.com/factsheets

Corporate Governance

Employment

Finance

General

IT & e-business

Law

Marketing

Strategy

Tax

**Law Society**

www.lawsociety.org.uk

Main London office: Law Society's Hall, 113 Chancery Lane, London WC2A 1PL

020 7242 1222

The Law Society is the regulatory and representative body for 116,000 solicitors in England and Wales, with public responsibilities including regulating and representing solicitors, supporting solicitors and influencing law reform.

The Society has a number of offices; check their website for the one nearest you.

**TEC International**

www.teconline.com (UK office, www.tecuk.co.uk)

UK office: One Crown Walk, Jewry Street, Winchester, Hampshire SO23 8BD

01962 841 188

TEC International helps companies outperform the competition. Business leaders come to TEC to accelerate the growth of their business and of themselves. Growth comes from one-to-one executive coaching, access to a group of trusted peers and entry into the worldwide network of more than 10,000 executives.

**UK Patent Office**
www.patent.gov.uk
Concept House, Cardiff Road, Newport, South Wales NP10 8QQ
0845 9 500 505
The UK Patent Office helps stimulate innovation and enhance the international competitiveness of British industry and commerce. It offers customers an accessible, high-quality, value-for-money system for granting intellectual property rights such as copyright, designs, patents and trademarks.

**www.dti.gov.uk**
**www.independentdirector.co.uk**
**www.ukonline.gov.uk**
**www.cbi.org.uk**
**www.icsa.org.uk**
**www.dti.gov.uk/cld/condocs/htm**

# Index